Smoothie
POWER

Robert Oser

Book Publishing Company
Summertown, Tennessee

Published in the United States by
Book Publishing Company
P.O. Box 99
Summertown, TN 38483
1-888-260-8458

Printed in the United States

ISBN 1-57067-177-X

10   09   08   07   06   05   6   5   4   3   2   1

Oser, Robert, 1948-
  Smoothie power / Robert Oser.
     p. cm.
  Includes index.
  ISBN 1-57067-177-X
  1. Blenders (Cookery) 2. Smoothies (Beverages) I. Title.

TX840.B5O78 2004
641.8'75–dc22
                          2004023794

Calculations for the nutritional analyses in this book are based on the average number of servings listed with the recipes and the average amount of an ingredient if a range is called for. Calculations are rounded up to the nearest gram. If two options for an ingredient are listed, the first one is used. Not included are fat used for frying (unless the amount is specified in the recipe), optional ingredients, or serving suggestions.

Listed from top to bottom.
Front cover: High C's Smoothie, p. 87, Black and Blue(Berry) Smoothie, p. 51
Back cover: Mango Lassi, p. 65, Triple-A Smoothie, p. 81,

Printed on recycled paper

The Book Publishing Co. is committed to preserving ancient forests and natural resources. We have elected to print this title on Torchglow Opaque, which is 30% postconsumer recycled and processed chlorine free. As a result of our paper choice, we have saved the following natural resources:

8 trees
378 lbs of solid waste
3425 gallons of net greenhouse gases
742 lbs of net greenhouse gases
1378 kw hours of electricity

BOOK
PUBLISHING
COMPANY

We are a member of Green Press Initiative. For more information about Green Press Initiative visit: www.greenpressinitiative.org

contents

INTRODUCTION 5

INGREDIENTS, EQUIPMENT, GENERAL TIPS 7

BREAKFAST SMOOTHIES 31

SIMPLE & ALL-FRUIT SMOOTHIES 39

EXOTIC SMOOTHIES FROM DISTANT LANDS 55

DAIRY & NONDAIRY MILK-BASED SMOOTHIES & FRAPPÉS 69

ATHLETIC BOOSTERS & HEALING SMOOTHIES 85

SHAKES & DESSERT SMOOTHIES 95

PARTY & HOLIDAY SHAKES 115

Introduction

IMAGINE FOR A MOMENT PREPARING A FOOD SO DELICIOUS THAT IT WILL PLEASE almost everyone, regardless of age, gender, religious or political affiliation, nationality or culture, occupation, or lifestyle. Imagine that this magical food is inexpensive to prepare, and doesn't need fancy or expensive equipment or time-consuming, labor-intensive techniques to prepare. Imagine also that it can be made by almost anyone—even a child—regardless of their culinary experience, usually in a matter of a few minutes, without cooking and little to no chopping (if you would rather not chop). This magical dish can be prepared from all raw ingredients, preserving all the nutrients and enzymes. It can easily be prepared without any animal ingredients. You needn't add any foods that may cause you an allergic reaction—no wheat, no gluten, no yeast. However, if you wish, you can add all sorts of nutritional "boosters"—wheat germ, bee pollen, spirulina, flaxseed oil, psyllium seed husks, you name it. Small children love it and will ask for more (and you won't mind giving it to them). Hard-to-please teenagers make their own, their way. Athletes enjoy them after a workout to replenish lost nutrients and calories. Harried students and workers enjoy them for a quick, nutritious breakfast. Body builders add extra protein, calories, and nutrients to theirs for "bulking up." For dieters, they can be made low-fat, low-calorie, and nutritious . . . or they can be gussied up as a very decadent or romantic dessert. Of course you know we're talking about smoothies, those wonderful, nutritious, refreshing drinks made so easily just by throwing a few ingredients into a blender.

The recipes in this book will provide you with the directions to create your own quick, delicious smoothies. There are smoothies for most any taste, occasion, or lifestyle. My family and I had a wonderful time creating these recipes and are confident you and your family and friends will enjoy them as much as we have.

I also hope that using these recipes ignites a spark of creativity that takes you beyond the recipes and into a realm of your own creation. After all, giving you my recipes is rather like giving you directions to my house. I urge you to create directions to your house, where your creativity dwells, where eating and preparing food is a personal art and, like a "Dada" puzzle, all the pieces fit anywhere you would like them to fit. Smoothies beg for creativity, freedom to play and experiment, sometimes to succeed, and sometimes to go back to the drawing board and try again. Because even the "failures" are usually pretty tasty, smoothies are a good place for someone who considers the kitchen unexplored territory to start on the path to delicious, nutritious eating.

Parents, please note that letting your children prepare their own smoothies (help or guide very young children) may often cause them to develop a lifelong interest in a healthy lifestyle. Because smoothies are so simple and the taste is so rewarding, making them builds confidence and the desire to do it again.

So, get out the blender and start filling it with delicious fruits and goodies! Call in the family and friends, and experience the refreshing goodness of smoothies!

Robert Oser

Ingredients

Naturally the most common ingredient in smoothies would be some type of fruit. Most of the recipes in this book feature at least one fruit.

Fresh Fruit and Frozen Fruit

Very freshly picked fruit, within a couple of hours of harvest, has the highest nutrient content and usually the best flavor. Some fruits, like bananas, need to ripen a while after harvest. As fruit sits around, it will begin to lose nutrients (vitamins and enzymes) and flavor. (Minerals are generally more stable.) Thus, it's a good idea to eat fruits and vegetables soon after purchase to get the greatest value and benefit.

If your market, natural food store, or co-op has a good buy on fresh, seasonal fruit, you might want to take advantage of the bargain and buy extra. Prepare (wash, peel, seed, chop, etc.) any fruit you don't feel you will eat in a day or two, place it in a freezer-safe plastic bag or container, and freeze it until ready to use. Freezing will preserve much of the nutrients, but the longer the fruit is frozen, the more it will begin to dry out and suffer "freezer burn." Try to use frozen fruit within a month or two at the most.

Either fresh or frozen fruit is perfectly acceptable for smoothies, whichever is in most optimal condition. If you use mostly frozen fruit or other frozen ingredients in your smoothie, it will be thicker and often resemble ice cream or sorbet. Sometimes this may be desirable; other times you may prefer your smoothie to be at room temperature. It's always your choice!

Many natural food stores and co-ops carry frozen organic fruit. These are also very good and much more convenient than fresh organic produce, but expensive. It's much cheaper to freeze your own fruit.

Canned fruit has generally lost most of its flavor and nutritional value and is best avoided unless nothing else is available.

DRIED FRUIT, SOAKED FRUIT, AND STEWED FRUIT

Organic dried fruits purchased in bulk are also a good bargain, though their price per pound may seem expensive. That's because they are actually concentrated fruits. Thus, each prune you eat is a whole plum and each piece of dried pear is generally half a pear. As fruit dries, it loses moisture and shrinks, but it still contains the same amount of flavor and most of the nutrients of fresh fruit. However, the balance of nutrients changes pretty drastically. For example, water-soluble vitamins, such as vitamin C, may be lost, but vitamin A may become more concentrated.

One of the advantages of dried fruits is that they will keep for several months stored in an airtight, bug-proof container in a cool, dark place. Dried fruits make a delicious snack, trail mix, or camping food, but they are generally too hard for smoothies (they are dried, after all), unless, that is, they are either soaked or stewed.

Soaking dried fruit is very simple and is preferable to stewing. Simply soak the dried fruit in enough filtered spring or distilled water to cover, usually for a couple of hours or until the fruit has soaked up most of the water and has become soft and pliable. The warmer the water, the more quickly the fruit will soak it up, but room temperature water is just fine.

Boiling water will cook the fruit and destroy some of the nutrients and enzymes. That's why stewing is recommended only when you're really in a hurry to rehydrate the dried fruit. To stew fruit, simply place the fruit in a saucepan with enough water to cover. Cover with a lid and bring the water just to a boil. Reduce the heat to simmer and continue to cook, stirring once or twice, for about 15 minutes or until the fruit is very soft and about doubled in size.

A nice alternative to soaking or stewing your dried fruit in water is to use fruit juice, usually apple or white grape juice. This will add a few nutrients, flavor, and quite a bit of sweetness.

Most fruits can be dried and many are available at natural food stores and co-ops. Avoid any that are sugared or contain preservatives such as sulfur dioxide. Sulfur dioxide is often used on commercial dried fruits to preserve the fresh color but can be quite dangerous to people who are sensitive to it. Unsulfured dried fruit may not look quite as pretty or colorful, but it usually has much more flavor. If you only buy organic dried fruit (and I highly urge you to), you needn't worry about sulfur.

Among the most popular dried fruits you will find are mangoes, bananas (the real dried bananas, not fried, sugared banana chips), papaya (watch for sugar), apples, cranberries, cherries, peaches, pears, kiwis, persimmons, apricots, raisins (grapes), currants (like tiny raisins), prunes (plums), coconut (shredded or in flakes), pineapple, figs, and dates.

Here are a few tips for buying, storing, and preparing some of the fruits (and a couple of vegetables) used in this book. If there are other fruits or ingredients common or indigenous to your area, feel free—no, encouraged—to incorporate them into your smoothies.

Note: Whether it's stated or not, I always suggest buying and using organic foods whenever possible. Organic foods may seem more expensive, but in the long run they are less costly for your budget as well as for the planet. Shop at your local co-op or natural food store. Support local farmers' markets and organic produce stands. Local or community-owned businesses are a better bet than large, commercial markets, even those that sell health food alongside the granola. Buy fresh fruits and vegetables whenever possible. When not possible, buy frozen foods over canned foods, since freezing retains more nutrients than canning.

Avoid irradiated, genetically altered, highly processed foods, or foods that might have been sprayed heavily with pesticides or other chemicals. How can you tell which foods have been irradiated or genetically altered? Generally, you can't with commercial brands at most supermarkets. You can only be fairly certain that your foods are safe if you have either grown them yourself or if you buy from a reputable organic farmer or gardener, or from a market or store that does not purchase questionable foods or ingredients.

WHAT TO LOOK FOR, HOW TO PREPARE, AND HOW TO STORE SELECTED FRUITS AND VEGETABLES

APPLES, PEARS

WHAT TO LOOK FOR: Buy a good, crisp variety: Gala, Granny Smith, and Golden Delicious are all good. Look for smooth, unbruised skin. Organic apples may not be as pretty or shiny as commercial apples (that shine on commercial apples is a wax), but the flavor is generally better. If you're like me and like the skin, with organic apples you don't have to worry about pesticides and wax.

TO PREPARE: Peel the apples if you like, then core and chop. If freezing for later use, people generally advise to squeeze a little lemon juice over the apples to keep them from discoloring. If you're only using the apples for smoothies, though, cosmetic perfection isn't that important. Place the cut apples in a freezer bag or container and freeze. Soaked dried apples are quite good in a smoothie, also. Or you might try unsweetened applesauce. Treat pears the same as apples, except pears will become soft and creamy when they ripen.

TO STORE: Apples and pears are generally best kept in a bowl on the table, where they are in plain sight and will be used often. Don't hide them in a refrigerator, as they will tend to lose their crispness and become mushy.

Apricots, peaches

What to look for: Bright, unblemished fruit with a fragrant smell. Apricots are at their peak when they are just beginning to soften.

To prepare: Halve or quarter and remove the pit. Apricots have a slightly fuzzy skin that some people don't like but, if you're not one of those people, leave apricots intact. The peel adds nutrients and flavor, and you won't notice it in a smoothie. Soaked dried apricots are wonderful in a smoothie, adding lots of beta-carotene, iron, and a wonderful flavor.

To store: Place in a fruit bowl, or refrigerate if fruit is not used in a couple of days.

Avocados

What to look for: Black, soft fruit (ripe) or green, hard fruit (unripe), without blemishes or bruises.

To prepare: Halve the ripened avocado and remove the large pit. Scoop the pulp out with a spoon. If not using right away, squeeze a little lemon or lime juice over to keep it from turning brown.

To store: If unripe, store in the fruit bowl. If ripe, use right away or store in the refrigerator to keep from over-ripening. To ripen rapidly, place the avocado in a paper bag with an apple. The apple will give off a gas that ripens the avocado very quickly.

Bananas

What to look for: Unblemished fruit. Most bananas are yellow and fairly large but some new varieties are hitting the markets that are smaller, sometimes red, and quite delicious. Tiny bananas like Manzanos (called apple bananas) are also becoming very popular.

To prepare: Simply peel and break the banana into pieces small enough to fit into your blender. Dried whole bananas are now available and, soaked or stewed, these make a wonderful addition to your smoothie. Bananas are very high in potassium.

To store: Bananas will keep very well in your fruit bowl until ready to use. As they ripen they begin to get dark spots that multiply until the skin becomes quite dark and very fragrant. Bananas are great for smoothies from the time they get their first spot until they become fairly dark and shriveled. Usually the more spots a banana has, the riper and sweeter it is. If it starts to become too ripe, peel the banana, place it in a freezer bag, and freeze it until needed.

Bilberries

What to look for: Bilberries are only beginning to become available. You may find them frozen or sometimes as a fruit jam or conserve. Bilberries are reported to be good for eyesight.

Blackberries, Blueberries, Raspberries, Boysenberries

What to look for: In season, blackberries will be plump and juicy. Avoid berries that show signs of mold or look old and spoiled.

To prepare: Sort through the berries and discard any that do not meet your approval. Otherwise, just rinse and throw them in!

To store: Refrigerate or freeze until needed. Do not wash raspberries until just before using, as they are delicate and will spoil faster after washing. Frozen organic blackberries are often available at your natural food store or co-op.

Cantaloupes, Honeydews

What to look for: Unblemished skin, slightly soft on the blossom end, with a definite pleasant aroma.

To PREPARE: Cut off both ends and stand the cantaloupe on one end. Peel by cutting down the sides, top to bottom. Halve the cantaloupe and scoop out the seeds with a spoon. Cut the cantaloupe into small chunks and use immediately, or refrigerate in a plastic container.

To STORE: Whole cantaloupe needs no refrigeration unless you prefer to eat it cold. Freeze any prepared cantaloupe you are not eating immediately.

CARROTS

WHAT TO LOOK FOR: Alright, I confess, a carrot is a vegetable, but it works so well in smoothies, either chopped (if you have a strong blender) or as fresh carrot juice. Look for firm, stiff carrots with no blemishes or bad spots.

To PREPARE: Juice or cut into small pieces. If you have a food processor, you can use it to grate them.

To STORE: Refrigerate.

CHERRIES

WHAT TO LOOK FOR: Look for plump, firm, but not hard fruit with a bright color. Avoid bruised fruit. Cherries with the stem still attached are best. Organic frozen cherries are usually readily available, as well.

To PREPARE: Cut cherries in half and remove the pit. (There is a contraption designed to pit cherries, but unless you're going to pit an awful lot of cherries, it's probably not worth buying.)

To STORE: Keep whole, unpitted cherries in a loose bag in the fruit drawer of your refrigerator. Once you've pitted the cherries, use them right away or freeze.

COCONUTS

WHAT TO LOOK FOR: Uncracked fruit with the liquid still inside (shake them to check). Young coconuts have a delectable, custard-like meat.

TO PREPARE: Use a heavy hammer or hatchet (seriously) to crack the coconut. I have a friend who uses a machete but, unless you're experienced in the use of a machete, I do not recommend it as a kitchen appliance. Scrape the coconut meat from the inside walls of the shell using a heavy spoon. Grate fresh coconut with the small holes of a hand grater, or buy dried coconut, shredded or in flakes. Coconut may be used raw or lightly toasted. If you would like to toast your coconut, just place grated coconut in a dry skillet (coconut has oil of its own) and cook, stirring, over medium heat until golden brown. Be careful not to burn.

TO STORE: Use fresh coconut right away. Dried coconut may be stored in a cool, dry place for several months.

CRANBERRIES

WHAT TO LOOK FOR: Plump, ripe berries. Usually they are available in one- or two-pound bags, and you can't really sort through and look for the best berries. Canned unsweetened or fruit-sweetened cranberry sauce works well in some recipes, as well.

TO PREPARE: Pour the cranberries into a bowl of water, and discard any that sink. Sort through the rest and throw away any that are shriveled, soft, or otherwise showing signs of spoilage.

TO STORE: Refrigerate or freeze until ready to use. Frozen organic cranberries are often found in natural food stores during the winter holidays.

Dates

WHAT TO LOOK FOR: Plump, soft dates with uniform, unblemished skin. Avoid chopped, dried date pieces. Those are best for cookies and date bread but not smoothies.

TO PREPARE: Halve and pit (if not already pitted), then chop the dates. To prevent your knife from becoming too caked with dried dates, rinse often in hot water.

TO STORE: Dried or fresh dates will store well in a plastic bag or container kept in a cool, dry place.

Figs

WHAT TO LOOK FOR: Figs may be purchased fresh when in season, but otherwise opt for dried figs. Fresh figs are usually light to dark green, sometimes with black or purple. They should be unblemished and only slightly soft. Dried figs are often available in different varieties, usually Black Mission (small, black, and very dry), Calimyrna (larger, plump, tan, and juicier) or Turkish (similar to Calimyrna but sometimes larger and sweeter).

TO PREPARE: Fresh figs should have their stems removed but are otherwise ready to use. Dried figs should be soaked or stewed.

TO STORE: Refrigerate fresh figs unless eating soon. Dried figs may be stored in a cool, dry place.

Grapes, Raisins

WHAT TO LOOK FOR: For smoothies, only use a seedless variety. (It's just too much effort to seed grapes.) Look for firm, clean fruit still attached to the stem. Dried grapes in the forms of raisins and currants (actually a different but related berry) are available in your favorite co-op and natural food store.

TO PREPARE: Sort through the grapes and discard any shriveled, moldy, or otherwise unacceptable fruit. Use immediately or freeze for later use. Raisins and currants should be soaked before using in smoothies; if not they will be a little chewy.

TO STORE: Refrigerate or store in a colander on your table until ready to use. I have a friend who keeps a colander of grapes on top of his refrigerator. Sometimes he forgets to eat them for a while and finds he has made raisins! Raisins and currants may be stored in a cool, dry place.

GRAPEFRUIT

WHAT TO LOOK FOR: Large, plump, fragrant, firm fruit with clear skin. Unless you have a pretty powerful blender, blended grapefruit (as well as oranges, tangerines, and tangelos) will be somewhat stringy. If you don't have a powerful blender, I recommend using grapefruit juice or frozen grapefruit juice concentrate instead.

TO PREPARE: If you think your blender can handle it, peel as you would the cantaloupe (remove as much of the white fiber as possible), remove any seeds, and section or chop the fruit. Freeze or use immediately.

TO STORE: Grapefruits keep very well without refrigeration and (I think) seem to get sweeter as they sit.

GUAVAS

WHAT TO LOOK FOR: Guavas, an oval-shaped fruit with a smooth green skin, are new to most areas of the United States. Usually you'll have to settle for guava nectar or juice.

TO PREPARE: If you can find fresh guavas, peel, halve, remove the seeds, and chop. Freeze the pulp or use right away.

TO STORE: Guavas will keep for a few days at room temperature, but refrigerate for longer storage.

KIWIS

WHAT TO LOOK FOR: Firm, well-shaped fruit without blemishes.

TO PREPARE: Kiwis have a soft, fuzzy brown skin. You may leave this on or peel, as you prefer. If you peel it, follow the same technique as for a cantaloupe. No need to remove the seeds as they are very small and no problem. Use the fruit immediately or freeze for later.

TO STORE: Kiwis will keep for two or three days without refrigeration, but refrigerate them for longer storage.

LEMONS

WHAT TO LOOK FOR: Large, firm fruit with a bright color. Lemon (and lime) juice is available in small bottles. It's not quite as good as fresh but will certainly work in a pinch.

TO PREPARE: Before juicing, roll the lemon on a hard counter or squeeze with your hands to break up the membrane on the inside and release more juice. Juice the lemon with a citrus juicer or by hand (hold it over a strainer). Use the juice right away or freeze for later.

TO STORE: Lemons store well at room temperature until ready to use.

LIMES

WHAT TO LOOK FOR, HOW TO PREPARE AND STORE: Same as lemons, except that limes are more difficult to juice by hand. Cut the lime in half and twist a fork in the lime half to break up the membranes. Limes don't have seeds so there's no need to squeeze over a strainer.

Mangoes

WHAT TO LOOK FOR: Ripe mangoes should have a smooth, reddish-orange skin and be slightly soft to the touch with a delightful aroma. Frozen mango or mango-orange juice concentrate is also popular.

TO PREPARE: It's rather tricky to cut a mango, as they tend to be quite stringy. The best way I have found is to set the oval-shaped fruit up on the long, narrow edge and halve the fruit (more or less) by cutting down the middle until hitting the large oval seed and then cutting down one side of the seed. Do the same on the other side of the seed. Cut each half into long narrow strips and cut the peel away from each strip. Chop and use or freeze for later.

TO STORE: Fresh mangoes will ripen well in the fruit bowl. If they begin to get too soft, store them in the refrigerator and use them soon.

Nectarines

WHAT TO LOOK FOR: Nectarines resemble a smooth-skinned peach. They should be firm to just becoming soft to the touch with a reddish-yellow unblemished skin and sweet fragrance.

TO PREPARE: Halve the fruit and remove the seed. (A spoon is safer for this task than a sharp knife.) Chop and use or freeze for later.

TO STORE: Nectarines will ripen well for a couple of days in the fruit bowl at room temperature, but keep an eye on them or they may suddenly become too ripe or spoil.

Oranges, Tangerines

WHAT TO LOOK FOR: Plump, round fruit without spots or blemishes or soft spots. Color is no indication of the quality of the fruit.

To prepare: As oranges (also grapefruit, tangerines, etc.) tend to be stringy, I normally juice them or use frozen orange juice concentrate. However, if you have a very powerful blender or are very careful to remove all the seeds and white membrane, it is possible to blend oranges.

To store: Oranges will store quite well for relatively long periods of time (sometimes weeks) without refrigeration. Another good prospect for the kitchen fruit bowl.

Papayas

What to look for: Papayas range in size from about the size of a small eggplant to very large fruit weighing several pounds. They will also vary in color, with different shades and mottled patterns of dark brown, green, red, and orange. Ripe papayas will give off a sweet, enticing fragrance.

To prepare: Peel and seed like a cantaloupe. Cut into small pieces and use right away or freeze them for later. Papayas are especially flavorful with a little lime juice squeezed over them.

To store: Papayas will keep for a couple of days without refrigeration, but once ripened or cut they should be eaten or refrigerated.

Passionfruit

What to look for: Not often available fresh in the United States. You usually have to settle for passionfruit juice or sorbet.

Persimmons

What to look for: Soft fruit without blemishes indicates ripeness.

To store: Ripen at room temperature, then store in the refrigerator.

Pineapples

WHAT TO LOOK FOR: Firm fruit that gives just slightly when squeezed, with no bruises and a wonderful fragrance. Frozen pineapple and frozen concentrated juice are also good to use.

TO PREPARE: Cut the top off with the leaves. If you stick the top in a pot of soil and water it, it will grow into a lovely plant (though it will be several years until you get a pineapple). Cut a flat bottom on the other end, and peel down the sides as with cantaloupe. Cut out any small "eyes" that you may have missed. Cut the peeled pineapple into quarters lengthwise, and remove the tough core. Chop and use or freeze for later.

TO STORE: Pineapple will store for a few days without refrigeration (depending upon its ripeness), but refrigerate, use, or freeze it as soon as it ripens.

Plums

WHAT TO LOOK FOR: Firm fruit just becoming soft to the touch, with a smooth, unwrinkled skin and no blemishes. Color and size will vary through the dozens of varieties of plums.

TO PREPARE: Halve and carefully remove the seed. Peel if desired; unless the peel is sour there's no need to remove it. Use or freeze for later.

TO STORE: Store at room temperature until ripe, then refrigerate.

Prunes

WHAT TO LOOK FOR: Dried, pitted prunes (plums).

TO PREPARE: Soak or stew prunes until soft.

TO STORE: Keep in a plastic bag or container in a cool, dry place.

Pumpkin

WHAT TO LOOK FOR: Though generally treated as a vegetable, pumpkin is actually a fruit. Look for a firm, unblemished fruit. Canned organic pumpkin is also readily available.

TO PREPARE: Peel (as with cantaloupe), halve, and scoop out the seeds with a spoon. Chop into one-inch cubes. Pumpkin is very hard so watch carefully that your knife does not slip. Steam or boil until tender.

TO STORE: Keep frozen until ready to prepare.

Rhubarb

WHAT TO LOOK FOR: Long pink to red stalks.

TO PREPARE: Rhubarb needs to be cooked before using. Cut the leaves from the stalks (if they're still attached) and discard the leaves (they are toxic). Cut the stalks into one-inch pieces, and stew until soft and tender. May be frozen after stewing.

TO STORE: Refrigerate or freeze until ready to prepare.

Strawberries

WHAT TO LOOK FOR: Fresh strawberries are bright red, firm, and aromatic. Avoid bruised, moldy, or pale fruit. Frozen strawberries are also good.

TO PREPARE: Remove the top leaves and the hard, white base of the leaves with a paring knife.

TO STORE: Keep frozen until ready to prepare.

Watermelon

What to look for: Similar to cantaloupe but usually larger and with seeds scattered throughout the pulp. Either remove the seeds or buy a seedless variety.

Yams, sweet potatoes

What to look for: Another vegetable that works especially well in smoothies. Look for firm flesh without blemishes or soft spots.

To prepare: Peel, if desired, and chop into small pieces. Steam or boil until tender. Use right away or freeze for later use.

Milk and Nondairy "Milks"

Many of the smoothies in this book use either a milk product (milk, ice cream, yogurt, buttermilk, cottage or ricotta cheese, etc.) or a dairy-free milk substitute for the same ingredient (soy, rice, almond, or oat beverage, soy yogurt, amazake, soy or rice frozen dessert, homemade nut "milk," or soft silken tofu). Most of these products are fairly interchangeable, so feel free to use whatever you like. Keep in mind that some will be thicker (tofu) and others thinner (dairy or nondairy milk). Some will be cold or frozen (ice cream or dairy-free frozen dessert).

Most are self-explanatory but here are descriptions and tips for using some of the more unusual products.

General Notes: There is a lot of controversy over the health benefits and dangers of dairy products. Suffice it to say that dairy products are cruel to dairy animals; they may be unhealthful (or at least not as nutritious as has been generally believed), and they are not necessary for a balanced diet. Soy- and rice-based products will substitute very nicely for most any dairy product. However, if you choose to use dairy products I recommend buying organic (naturally) and limiting your intake of them. Keep an eye on the fat content of the products you use (that goes for dairy-free substitutes as well). Avoid the higher fat products or use a lower fat version.

BUTTERMILK: Low-fat, cultured skim milk. Adds a nice sour flavor and a healthful bacteria culture (similar to yogurt).

KEFIR: A cultured, flavored milk, much like a liquid, drinkable yogurt.

NONFAT MILK POWDER: Add water to reconstitute into liquid milk, or add as a supplement to increase nutrients, add flavor, or thicken.

YOGURT: Only buy yogurt containing live cultures, and watch for artificial flavors and gelatin.

SOYMILK, RICE MILK, OAT MILK, AND ALMOND MILK: The American Dairy Association, I know, objects to using the word milk to describe nondairy "milk-like" beverages, but for the sake of convenience, it just makes things easier. So, with apologies to the dairy business, these nondairy "milks," made from soy, rice, oats, and almonds, are great substitutes for those who are trying to avoid dairy, whether for medical reasons (lactose intolerance or other allergies), political reasons (environmental and ecological), or philosophical or ethical reasons (animal rights). The taste is similar to cow's milk (sometimes better). They are convenient to use, and most will substitute very well for traditional dairy products. Those products in aseptic packaging store easily and need no refrigeration until they are opened. Soymilk and rice milk also come in a powdered form similar to nonfat milk powder.

Like dairy products, these substitutes come in full-fat, low-fat (similar to 2% milk), and nonfat (similar to skim milk). There are plain varieties, as well as flavors such as vanilla, chocolate, carob, strawberry, or coffee. Many products are enriched to contain calcium, vitamins A and D, and other nutrients.

Besides milk substitutes, there are nondairy products manufactured to resemble ice cream, yogurt, cheese, and so on.

A few other products, while not specifically made to be used in place of dairy, resemble some of the traits of dairy products (texture, flavor, etc.) and will work very well in their place. Soft silken tofu (a very smooth form of tofu that blends especially well) and amazake make great dairy substitutes. Amazake, a sweet rice drink with other flavors added, is about the consistency of thick milk and adds a very nice flavor. It is very digestible and nutritious.

Coconut milk is not the thin, watery liquid from the center of fresh coconuts. It is made from water and coconut meat that has been soaked in hot water or boiled, then strained. Conveniently, it can be purchased in cans in most supermarkets and is available in both full-fat and low-fat varieties. Coconut milk may be substituted for milk and has the extra benefit of giving your smoothie a delightful coconut flavor.

Sweeteners

Agave Nectar: Made from the agave plant, agave nectar is very sweet but, like brown rice syrup, creates less havoc with blood sugar levels.

Brown Rice Syrup: A good substitute for honey, brown rice syrup is thick and sweet with a mild, pleasant flavor. Brown rice syrup is usually gentler on your blood sugar levels than either sugar or honey. It's available at any natural food store or co-op.

Blackstrap Molasses: The only truly nutritious sweetener (besides fresh, whole fruit), blackstrap is high in nutrients, especially calcium and iron. It also has a very strong taste, so don't let it overpower the other flavors.

Fruit Juice Concentrate: Those cans of frozen juice concentrate that you normally pour into a pitcher and mix with three cans of water actually make very good sweetening/flavoring agents. When thawed, they will keep for about a month in the refrigerator. Undiluted, they work very well to sweeten foods while adding an intense fruit flavor. Fruit juice concentrates come in many flavors; those most commonly used in smoothies are apple, orange, or pineapple. Feel free to try other flavors.

SmoothiePOWER

GRANULATED SUGAR CANE JUICE OR SUGAR CANE CRYSTALS: White, brown, and turbinado sugars are basically empty calories with little or no nutrients. Sugar cane products (such as Sucanat, Florida Crystals, etc.) are processed by juicing sugar cane and then dehydrating the juice, different than the method used to get regular granulated sugar. The resultant crystals are as sweet as sugar (and, unfortunately, affect your blood sugar the same way) but at least contain some vitamins, minerals, and enzymes. They are found under several brand names at natural food stores and co-ops.

HONEY: Buy only pure, raw, organic honey. It is more flavorful than sugar, and you generally need only about half as much to flavor and sweeten. Hard-core vegans do not eat honey out of respect for the bees.

MAPLE SYRUP: Avoid "maple-flavored" syrups; they are mostly corn syrup. Buy only pure, organic maple syrup. Grade B usually has a stronger flavor than grade A.

SORBET: A highly concentrated and flavorful frozen dessert, sorbets are mostly made from fruit and can be used to flavor or sweeten smoothies.

FLAVORINGS

EXTRACTS: Concentrated flavorings made by distilling plants and spices. Extracts come in a variety of flavors and generally contain alcohol or glycerin as a base. They will last indefinitely on your kitchen shelf.

FRESH GINGER ROOT: Usually found in the produce department, this aromatic root adds a delightful flavor and aroma when minced, grated, or juiced. (Also used as a folk remedy for nausea and motion sickness.)

MALT POWDER: A malted grain powder found in larger supermarkets or specialty shops, malt powder adds that special flavor that makes a "malt" what it is.

SPICES AND SEASONINGS: Cinnamon, nutmeg, cloves, allspice, spearmint, peppermint, chamomile, etc., all add a nice flavor when used sparingly.

Vanilla Beans: Found as dried whole beans in the natural food store or co-op, you can either chop or grind them for flavor. If you can place several vanilla beans in a bottle of brandy or vodka and let it sit, it will become vanilla extract.

Nutritional Additives

Bee Pollen: Rich in protein, B vitamins, and trace minerals, this healthful additive can cause problems for those who are allergic or sensitive to it. If you suspect you may have an allergy, begin with only a granule or two and see if you have any adverse reactions before taking more.

Chili Powders, Chiles, Cayenne: Add a little spice and zip where needed.

Flaxseeds and Flaxseed Oil: These seeds are high in beneficial omega-3 and omega-6 fatty acids. Adding either several tablespoons of whole flaxseeds or a spoonful of the oil to your smoothie will enrich your diet with these nutrients.

Herbs: Gingko biloba, ginseng, echinacea, goldenseal, and St. John's wort may be added as medicinal supplements, especially under a nutritionist's supervision.

Oat or Wheat Bran: Adds beneficial fiber.

Protein Powders: Though protein is seldom a problem in the United States, these powders can add needed protein for those who are deficient and will definitely add a nice flavor and thickness to your smoothies.

Psyllium Seed Husks: Very high in fiber, psyllium seed husks add bulk and promote regularity. The main ingredient of Metamucil is psyllium seed husks.

Spirulina: A highly nutritious dried blue-green algae, spirulina is rich with protein and lots of minerals, including hard-to-get trace minerals. It is also a wonderful antioxidant.

WHEAT GERM: Wheat germ is rich in protein, antioxidants, iron, and vitamin E. It also adds a little fiber, thickness, and flavor.

OTHER INGREDIENTS

CAROB POWDER AND CAROB CANDIES: Carob tastes similar (but not the same) to chocolate. It contains more nutrients and none of the harmful ingredients of chocolate, such as caffeine, theobromine, and oxalic acid. Carob comes from a bean in the locust family and is the Biblical "locusts and honey" that Jesus and St. John enjoyed.

CHAI TEA: A Middle Eastern drink made from black tea, spices, and sweetened milk, chai tea is very popular in teahouses and around college campuses. You can buy the ingredients and make your own chai tea, or you can buy chai tea already prepared (and sometimes caffeine-free).

COCOA POWDER AND CHOCOLATE: Buy only a good organic cocoa powder or chocolate. The better the quality, the better the flavor.

COFFEE: Use organic powdered instant or strongly brewed coffee to flavor your smoothies. Choose either regular caffeinated coffee or decaf, as you prefer.

FRUIT JUICES: Fresh or frozen juices add fruit flavor and make the smoothie thinner when it is getting too thick. I recommend using organic, raw, unfiltered juices with no sugars or sweeteners added.

GRAIN BEVERAGE: These are usually made from roasted barley and chicory. Grain beverages add a coffee-like flavor without the caffeine and tannins found in coffee.

GREEN TEA: Lower in caffeine than black tea and rich in healthful antioxidants, green tea comes in many varieties.

NATURAL SODAS: The wide variety of natural sodas on the market generally do not contain the caffeine and artificial ingredients found in commercial sodas. I think they have a more natural flavor.

NUTS AND SEEDS: Cashews, pecans, walnuts, almonds, hazelnuts (filberts), pine nuts, brazil nuts, peanuts (not actually a nut, but used as one), sunflower seeds, sesame seeds, etc., may be added for flavor, texture, or nutritional value. They provide protein, minerals, and healthy oils.

NUT BUTTERS: Peanut butter, cashew butter, almond butter, tahini (sesame seed butter), etc., may be used along with or in place of nuts.

ROSE WATER: Found in natural food stores and Middle Eastern markets, rose water adds a traditional flavor to lassis and other ethnic Mediterranean or Indian dishes.

WHITE CHOCOLATE: Many natural food stores, co-ops and gourmet specialty stores carry white chocolate or white chocolate chips. It is much sweeter than regular chocolate and has a unique flavor.

EQUIPMENT AND TECHNIQUES

Very simply, you will need a good blender, and possibly a knife and cutting board. Measuring cups or spoons might come in handy but are not essential (especially as most blender canisters have measurement marks on them). Freezer bags are handy for freezing leftover fresh fruit. A long-handled wooden or plastic spoon is handy for stirring the smoothie or removing it from the blender. (Turn the motor off when stirring! Splinters from the wooden spoon are not acceptable dietary fiber!) It's a wonderful idea to keep a couple of tall glasses or goblets in the freezer for serving ice-cold smoothies. That's about it!

As far as blenders go, there are many models on the market. Expect to pay between $25 and $40 for a good one. Look for a model with variable speeds and a good strong motor (cheap motors tend to burn out quickly). Beyond that, any other choices (color, size, etc.) are a matter of personal preference. The only other real consideration is if you want a glass or a plastic canister. Some people prefer a glass canister to prevent the leaching of plastic into the smoothie; others feel the glass canister is too heavy and unwieldy. In a pinch, a food processor will work in place of a blender, but since blenders are usually cheaper than food processors, I would not go out and buy a food processor just to make smoothies.

My fiance, a wonderful yard sale and bargain shopper, found a great Vita-Mix machine at a yard sale for $25. It does everything a blender will do but has an extra-strong motor for grinding wheat, kneading bread dough, making soup and ice cream, and a dozen other functions. I'm not saying you need a machine that does all that, and I don't often recommend used blenders (they're usually worn out), but if you're alert to bargains you can occasionally find some pretty good buys if you look around a while.

I find a good chef's or French knife to be the most efficient tool for chopping fruit. I sometimes use a serrated knife for very soft fruit and a paring knife for coring and detail work. However, any knife that feels comfortable to you will work. Use a spoon for removing seeds and pits.

I use a wooden cutting board. Never use the same cutting board that you use for chicken or meat to prepare your smoothie ingredients, or you run the risk of cross-contamination with bacteria. It also may not be a good idea to cut apples, say, on the same surface you just used to chop garlic.

When placing your ingredients in the blender, start with the liquid ingredients, then add the more solid fruit and such. Start your blender on a low speed to chop, and then turn it up to a higher speed at the end to blend and whip the ingredients. Sometimes your smoothie will become too thick, especially if you're using mostly frozen or drier ingredients, and the motor will strain. Turn the motor off and, using a long-handled spoon, stir the ingredients from the bottom to loosen. Remove the spoon and restart the blender.

TIPS AND NOTES ABOUT THE RECIPES

To make any smoothie colder, thicker, or to extend it, simply add ice cubes or crushed ice (depending on the strength of your blender). You might also add more flavor by freezing cubes of juice, milk, or other ingredients. Store these cubes in plastic bags in your freezer, and simply toss in a couple or a cupful, as you desire. Sometimes the recipes will call for ice as an ingredient. Always feel free to experiment with other frozen cubes.

I generally keep a couple of frosted glasses and beer mugs in my freezer. They're great for smoothies, root beer floats, whatever! When you wash and rinse the glass, just put it straight into the freezer. Don't dry the glass, because the water turns to frost!

Tips on preparing specific ingredients are found at the end of some of the recipes.

NOTES ON NUTRITIONAL ANALYSES

The nutritional analyses for these recipes are based on using 2% milk when dairy milk is called for and low-fat yogurt when yogurt of any flavor is called for. If you are not using dairy products, be sure that you use calcium-fortified soymilk in order to achieve comparable calcium amounts.

Breakfast
SMOOTHIES

TahitianSunriseTropical
BreakfastSMOOTHIE

2 servings

What a great way to wake up! This rich, satisfying smoothie will give you a jump-start on your day.

> **2 mangoes*, peeled and chopped**
> **1 cup fresh orange juice**
> **1 cup coconut milk (fresh or canned)**
> **Juice of 1 lime**
> **1 tablespoon flaxseed oil (optional)**

Blend all ingredients together very, very well (mangoes tend to be stringy), and serve in a tall, frosted glass. Enjoy!

Per serving: Calories 431,
Protein 4 g, Fat 26 g, Carbohydrates 53 g,
Fiber 7 g, Calcium 57 mg, Sodium 21 mg

*TIP: When fresh mangoes are out of season or hard to obtain, cut dried mango into small pieces and soak in water for ½ hour to hydrate. One-half cup of soaked mango will equal 1 fresh mango. This works with any other dried fruit, such as papaya, pineapple, apples, and figs.

VARIATIONS

Substitute fresh pineapple for the mango when in season.

Substitute yogurt for the coconut milk.

Add a handful of raw cashews before blending.

Some might like to add 1 tablespoon protein powder or 1 teaspoon bee pollen.

FuzzyNavelSMOOTHIE

servings

This sweet, refreshing smoothie can be made with fresh or frozen peaches. I don't like to remove the peel (I think it gives them "appeal"), but if you don't like the fuzziness, go ahead and peel the peach. The cashews really add a smooth richness.

> **2 large or 3 small peaches, seeded**
> **1 cup frozen orange juice concentrate**
> **½ cup cashews**
> **2 tablespoons protein powder (optional)**

Blend the orange juice and cashews until very smooth. Add the rest of the ingredients, and blend again. Serve in a tall glass and enjoy!

Per serving: Calories 499,
Protein 10 g, Fat 18 g, Carbohydrates 81 g,
Fiber 5 g, Calcium 69 mg, Sodium 10 mg

VARIATIONS

Substitute papaya juice for all or part of the orange juice.

Soak ½ cup almonds in distilled water for 2 days and use in place of cashews. You'll be surprised what the soaking does for the flavor and digestibility of the almonds.

Strawberry-Kiwi
FRAPPÉ

2 servings

Yum! This cool, refreshing smoothie will open your eyes in the morning with a jolt of intense flavor. The rest of the day just has to be wonderful when it starts with this!

- **1 cup frozen strawberries**
- **2 kiwis, chopped, peeling optional**
- **2 frozen bananas**
- **1 cup frozen apple juice concentrate**
- **1 tablespoon wheat germ**
- **1 tablespoon flaxseeds or oil**
- **1 tablespoon bee pollen**

Blend everything until smooth and creamy. Serve and enjoy!

Per serving: Calories 480, Protein 4 g,
Fat 9 g, Carbohydrates 103 g,
Fiber 9 g, Calcium 67 mg, Sodium 41 mg

VARIATIONS

Substitute orange juice concentrate for apple.

Substitute yogurt or buttermilk for the apple juice concentrate.

MochaCOOLER

If you like the flavor of mocha, you'll love this creamy cooler. And if you prefer, you can do it caffeine-free!

> **2 cups brewed coffee (regular or decaf) or grain beverage, cooled**
> **1 cup dairy or dairy-free milk**
> **2 tablespoons cocoa or carob powder**
> **1 cup ice**

Blend all ingredients well and serve in a frosted glass with a cinnamon stick or a dollop of whipped cream. Enjoy!

Per serving: Calories 78, Protein 5 g,
Fat 3 g, Carbohydrates 10 g,
Fiber 2 g, Calcium 160 mg, Sodium 67 mg

Coffee-DateSMOOTHIE

*2*servings

Use soft dates like Medjools or Black Sphinx, and chop first so they don't clog the blender. This is a delightful breakfast smoothie that will give you extra motivation to get up and going. Just blend and enjoy!

> **2 (8-ounce) containers coffee-flavored yogurt**
> **1 cup dairy or dairy-free milk, yogurt, or buttermilk**
> **⅓ cup chopped soft dates**
> **1 cup ice**
> **2 tablespoons honey or maple syrup (optional)**

Per serving: Calories 343, Protein 15 g,
Fat 5 g, Carbohydrates 61 g,
Fiber 2 g, Calcium 556 mg, Sodium 222 mg

CinnamonRoll SMOOTHIE

2 servings

This versatile smoothie may be served either for a quick, delicious breakfast or as a rich dessert. It's a winner either way!

¼ cup raisins
¼ cup rolled oats
¼ cup dried apple slices
1½ cups apple juice
1 cup oat or almond milk
½ cup pecans
½ teaspoon cinnamon

Soak the raisins, oats, and dried apple slices in the apple juice overnight to soften. Blend all ingredients together well and enjoy!

Per serving: Calories 434, Protein 6 g,
Fat 21 g, Carbohydrates 62 g,
Fiber 7 g, Calcium 40 mg, Sodium 21 mg

PB&J SMOOTHIE

2 servings

Comfort food for the inner child, for sure! Yummy! Blend ingredients and serve in a tall, chilled glass.

2 cups dairy or dairy-free milk or yogurt
1 cup frozen Concord grape juice concentrate
2 frozen bananas
½ cup peanut butter
1 tablespoon wheat germ
½ cup ice (optional)

Per serving: Calories 876, Protein 29 g,
Fat 34 g, Carbohydrates 118 g,
Fiber 9 g, Calcium 364 mg, Sodium 283 mg

SmoothiePOWER

PowerBreakfast
SMOOTHIE

2 servings

This may well be the real breakfast of champions. This power-packed smoothie will really get you up and goin' in the morning!

- **1 cup strong green tea**
- **1 teaspoon instant ginseng tea**
- **2 frozen bananas**
- **½ cup frozen strawberries**
- **1 cup frozen apple or orange juice concentrate**
- **2 tablespoons wheat germ**
- **2 tablespoons flaxseeds or oil**
- **1 tablespoon spirulina**
- **1 teaspoon bee pollen**

Blend together well and enjoy! (Don't forget your vitamins!)

Per serving: Calories 424, Protein 5 g,
Fat 5 g, Carbohydrates 94 g,
Fiber 7 g, Calcium 72 mg, Sodium 39 mg

PeachCappuccino
SMOOTHIE

2 servings

Better than a frothy cappuccino. If you don't care for caffeine, try it with decaf or a grain beverage. There are several options in your natural food store or co-op!

1 cup frozen peaches

1 cup dairy or dairy-free yogurt or milk (if using yogurt, try cappuccino or mocha flavor)

½ cup peach juice

3 tablespoons instant coffee (regular or decaf) or grain beverage

1 cup ice

½ teaspoon vanilla or other natural flavor, such as butterscotch, mint, coconut, hazelnut, etc. (optional)

Place all ingredients in a blender, and blend well until smooth and frothy. Serve, garnished with a mint sprig, pansy blossom, and/or a cinnamon stick. Enjoy!

Per serving: Calories 190, Protein 7 g,
Fat 2 g, Carbohydrates 38 g,
Fiber 1 g, Calcium 217 mg, Sodium 90 mg

TIP: Many flowers (pansies, nasturtiums, violets, etc.) are edible and make beautiful (and simple) garnishes.

VARIATIONS

Substitute apricots or mangoes for the peaches.

Add a pinch of cinnamon or nutmeg.

Simple & All-Fruit SMOOTHIES

Avo-Banana Whip

This unusual smoothie is delicious, and packed with nutrients. The kiwi and strawberries add a nice sweet-tart flavor that harmonizes well with the avocado and bananas.

> **1 large avocado, peeled and seeded**
> **2 frozen bananas**
> **1 kiwi, peeled**
> **½ cup frozen strawberries**
> **1 cup apple juice or kefir (liquid yogurt)**
> **2 tablespoons honey or brown rice syrup**
> **Juice of 1 lime (optional)**
> **½ cup ice (optional)**

Blend all ingredients together until smooth. Serve in a tall glass and enjoy!

Per serving: Calories 423, Protein 4 g,
Fat g, Carbohydrates 74 g,
Fiber 11 g, Calcium 43 mg, Sodium 18 mg

Orange-Tangerine Smoothie

2 servings

Very simple but oh, so refreshing! Blend all the ingredients well, and enjoy this often!

> **2 cups tangerine juice**
> **1 cup orange juice**
> **1 cup ice**

Per serving: Calories 162, Protein 2 g,
Fat 1 g, Carbohydrates 38 g,
Fiber 1 g, Calcium 58 mg, Sodium 4 mg

Tooty-Fruity SMOOTHIE

3 servings

You'll go bananas (and oranges and apples) for this fruity cooler. Don't worry about the recipe, though; just use any fruit that is readily available. They're all good. If you use all frozen fruit and juice, the smoothie will be very thick. Serve it in a bowl with a spoon, perhaps.

> **1 cup frozen strawberries**
> **2 frozen bananas**
> **1 cup frozen orange juice concentrate**
> **1 cup frozen grape juice concentrate**
> **1 cup frozen apple juice concentrate**

Blend all the ingredients together well.

Per serving: Calories 562, Protein 4 g,
Fat 1 g, Carbohydrates 138 g,
Fiber 4 g, Calcium 73 mg, Sodium 34mg

Tamarind SMOOTHIE

2 servings

Tamarinds are an unusual fruit with a unique flavor. They can often be found in Asian or Indian markets and sometimes in Mexican markets as well. The flavor blends very well with apple juice, and the tartness of the lemon (or lime) complements the flavor as well. Very refreshing on a hot day!

> **1 cup frozen tamarind pulp**
> **2 cups frozen apple juice concentrate**
> **¼ cup lemon or lime juice**

Blend together well and serve in a chilled glass.

Per serving: Calories 481, Protein 2 g,
Fat 1 g, Carbohydrates 120 g,
Fiber 1 g, Calcium 61 mg, Sodium 71 mg

Tucson TONIC

2 servings

What a wonderful, simple way to brighten up your morning!

> **Juice of 4 oranges (1 cup juice)**
> **1 large mango, peel and seed removed, or dried mango**
> **soaked in water (see page 32)**
> **1 cup raw, unfiltered apple juice**
> **2 orange slices (for garnish)**

Blend together the first three ingredients until smooth and frothy. Garnish with orange slices and serve.

Per serving: Calories 215, Protein 2 g,
Fat 1 g, Carbohydrates 54 g,
Fiber 4 g, Calcium 38 mg, Sodium 8 mg

VARIATIONS

Add, perhaps, a tablespoon protein powder or a teaspoon flaxseed oil.

For an icy cold, chunky smoothie, substitute ½ cup apple juice concentrate for the apple juice, and add ½ cup ice.

CodeRed SMOOTHIE

2 servings

No danger here! Just a wonderful sparkling, berry-flavored cooler. Place all ingredients in the blender, and process until smooth. This works fine with other frozen fruit and/or soda flavors. If you add a light white wine or champagne, it becomes a great drink for adult parties. Serve and enjoy!

> **1 cup frozen raspberries**
> **1 cup frozen strawberries**
> **1 (12-ounce) can raspberry flavored natural soda**

Per serving: Calories 132, Protein 1 g,
Fat 1 g, Carbohydrates 32 g,
Fiber 6 g, Calcium 24 mg, Sodium 1 mg

'50sFruitSalad
SMOOTHIE

2servings

Back in the 1950s, as a young boomer being brought up on "Good Housekeeping," I used to think that canned fruit salad (with little marshmallows) must be one of the four food groups. This delicious smoothie uses fresh ingredients and is a wonderful improvement, especially without the marshmallows. For thicker, richer, icier smoothies, freeze the fresh fruit first. Enjoy often!

2 apples, cored and chopped, peeled or not

2 fresh peaches, pitted, peeled or not

1 frozen banana, peeled

1 cup seedless grapes or frozen Concord grape juice concentrate

2 cups frozen orange juice concentrate

1 cup ice (if using fresh fruit)

Blend everything well and serve in frosted mugs, perhaps with a sprig of fresh mint. Enjoy!

Per serving: Calories 652, Protein 9 g,
Fat 2 g, Carbohydrates 161 g,
Fiber 10 g, Calcium 115 mg, Sodium 10 mg

VARIATIONS

Add honey or maple syrup to taste, or try a pinch of nutmeg or cardamom.

Strange as it may sound, just a drop of balsamic vinegar will bring out more of the natural sugars and make the fruit taste sweeter. Don't use too much, as you don't want the fruit to taste vinegary. You can mix it with ½ teaspoon vanilla.

Substitute 1 cup applesauce for the apples.

Add 1 cup coconut milk, almond (or other) milk, or ice cream.

Pirate'sParrot JUICE

Can't get your kids to eat carrots? Try this flavorful drink and see if they don't clamor for more. Simple and sweet, it's a treat for your whole family.

> **2 cups fresh pear juice (or 1 cup fresh pears chopped, peeling optional, plus 1 cup apple juice)**
> **1 cup fresh carrot juice**
> **1 cup ice**

Blend the ingredients well and serve with a sprig of mint.

Per serving: Calories 156, Protein 2 g,
Fat 1 g, Carbohydrates 38 g,
Fiber 3 g, Calcium 47 mg, Sodium 39 mg

VARIATIONS

Apple or most any other juice may be substituted for the pear, but the combination of pear and carrot is surprisingly delicious. I've also made this with good results using pineapple juice.

Add dairy or dairy-free yogurt or buttermilk.

RubyTuesday SMOOTHIE

2 servings

You'll treasure this sweet, fruity smoothie, but don't be greedy. Share the wealth! Blend the ingredients together and enjoy.

> **1 cup frozen raspberries**
> **1 cup frozen strawberries**
> **1 cup frozen cherries**
> **1 cup cranberry juice**

Per serving: Calories 165, Protein 2 g,
Fat 1 g, Carbohydrates 39 g,
Fiber 8 g, Calcium 43 mg, Sodium 11 mg

Persimmon-Cinnamon
SMOOTHIE

2 servings

Our local co-op gets so many persimmons every fall that they ripen before all of them can be sold. Here's a wonderfully delicious way to use those ripe persimmons—great for an autumn event or party.

1 cup fresh, ripe persimmons
1 cup apple juice
1 teaspoon ground cinnamon
1 cup ice

Blend all the ingredients well and serve in a tall, chilled glass!

Per serving: Calories 235, Protein 2 g,
Fat 1 g, Carbohydrates 61 g,
Fiber 9 g, Calcium 29 mg, Sodium 6 mg

VARIATIONS

Use 2 cups frozen apple juice concentrate instead of the apple juice and ice.

Substitute orange juice or concentrate for the apple.

Add 1 or 2 tablespoons maple syrup, if your persimmons are tart.

Pear-BilberrySMOOTHIE   *2* servings

Bilberries are becoming easier to find in co-ops and natural food stores, but if they're unavailable in your area, you might substitute blackberries or raspberries. Sometimes you might find bilberry jam. That will work well but is more concentrated, so try adding a few more ice cubes.

> **1 cup frozen bilberries (or other berries)**
> **1 frozen banana**
> **1 cup ice**
> **1 cup pear juice**
> **1 tablespoon honey or brown rice syrup (optional)**

Blend all ingredients together well and serve. Enjoy!

Per serving: Calories 151, Protein 1 g,
Fat 1 g, Carbohydrates 38 g,
Fiber 3 g, Calcium 19 mg, Sodium 11 mg

WatermelonSMOOTHIE   *2* servings

This refreshing summertime cooler can also be made with cantaloupe, honeydew, or other melons.

> **3 cups melon, peeled, seeded, and chopped**
> **1 cup frozen apple or white grape juice concentrate**

Blend ingredients well and enjoy!

Per serving: Calories 310, Protein 2 g,
Fat 2 g, Carbohydrates 75 g,
Fiber 2 g, Calcium 47 mg, Sodium 40 mg

Figgy-Figgy SMOOTHIE

The only thing I knew about figs when I was growing up was that they were put into cookie filling. I was in my twenties before I discovered the pleasures of fresh and dried figs. What a yummy fruit! If fresh figs are unavailable, simply soak some dried figs until soft.

> 1 cup fresh or soaked figs
> 1 fresh peach or 2 fresh apricots, seeded, peeling optional
> 1 fresh apple, cored and chopped, peeling optional
> 2 cups frozen apple juice concentrate
> 1 tablespoon wheat germ
> Pinch of cinnamon (optional)

Place all the ingredients into a blender, and blend until smooth.

Per serving: Calories 729, Protein 5 g,
Fat 3 g, Carbohydrates 181 g,
Fiber 11 g, Calcium 172 mg, Sodium 79 mg

VARIATIONS

Substitute or add a few soaked prunes, raisins, or dates.

Frozen white grape juice concentrate will substitute well for the apple juice.

Pistachio-Banana
SMOOTHIE

2 servings

This delicious smoothie takes more time, admittedly (you have to shell the pistachios, after all), but is well worth the extra effort. If pistachios are unavailable or you're feeling tired, substitute pine nuts or hazelnuts. (But be sure to try the pistachios sometime.)

3 frozen bananas
½ cup shelled pistachios
2 cups frozen apple juice concentrate
1 tablespoon wheat germ

Blend all the ingredients well and enjoy!

Per serving: Calories 1,074, Protein 20 g,
Fat 39 g, Carbohydrates 176 g,
Fiber 14 g, Calcium 170 mg, Sodium 77 mg

VARIATIONS

Add a handful of frozen strawberries or cherries.

Add a scoop of dairy or dairy-free frozen dessert or yogurt.

Substitute your favorite sorbet for the frozen apple juice concentrate.

Apricot-Nectarine
SMOOTHIE

2 servings

Apricots and nectarines go together so well—the staccato immediacy of the apricots and the laid-back smoothness of the nectarines. Like smooth jazz. Yin and yang harmony and percussion. Cool.

1 cup frozen apricots
1 cup frozen nectarines
2 frozen bananas
1 cup apple juice

Blend all the ingredients together and enjoy!

Per serving: Calories 299, Protein 5 g,
Fat 2 g, Carbohydrates 73 g,
Fiber 9 g, Calcium 49 mg, Sodium 7 mg

VARIATIONS

Try other fruit combinations: apricots and peaches, nectarines and peaches, apricots and mangoes, etc.

Perhaps you might prefer orange juice to the apple juice.

Apricot-Almond-Orange Smoothie

The almonds add a very nice flavor and lots of nutrients. If you forget to soak them, you might just substitute almond milk in a pinch.

> **1 cup frozen, rehydrated dried, or fresh apricots, peeling optional**
> **½ cup almonds, soaked for 2 days in 1 cup apple juice (add the apple juice as well)**
> **1 cup frozen orange juice concentrate**

Blend all the ingredients well and enjoy!

Per serving: Calories 544, Protein 12 g,
Fat 21 g, Carbohydrates 85 g,
Fiber 7 g, Calcium 166 mg, Sodium 13 mg

VARIATIONS

Coconut milk makes a tasty addition.

Try tossing in a pinch of nutmeg.

BlackandBlue(Berry)
SMOOTHIE

2 servings

Dark and rich, sensual and exotic, and not for people who like to play it safe. Step out a little, take deep breaths, and live life on the edge.

1 cup frozen blackberries
1 cup frozen blueberries
1 cup apple juice
2 frozen bananas
1 tablespoon wheat germ

Blend all the ingredients until smooth and thick.
Enjoy!

Per serving: Calories 265, Protein 3 g,
Fat 2 g, Carbohydrates 65 g,
Fiber 9 g, Calcium 43 mg, Sodium 10 mg

VARIATIONS

Substitute frozen raspberries or peaches.

Add or substitute almond milk for an interesting flavor.

Guava-Passion
SMOOTHIE

2 servings

Guava and passionfruit are both popular in other parts of the world but are just becoming familiar in the United States. If you can find fresh fruit, I urge you to try it. Sometimes you can find frozen fruit or juice. Use whatever is available and adjust the recipe accordingly. Hibiscus petals can be found in most natural food stores and co-ops and can be steeped as a tea. Just blend the ingredients until smooth and enjoy!

1 cup frozen guava
1 cup frozen passionfruit
1 cup raw, unfiltered apple juice
1 cup strong hibiscus tea

Per serving: Calories 127, Protein 1 g, Fat 1 g,
Carbohydrates 31 g, Fiber 5 g, Calcium 42 mg, Sodium 8 mg

Honeydew-Mint COOLER

2 servings

Sparkling and light, with just a hint of ginger, this will cool the hottest day!

1 cup frozen honeydew melon
2 frozen bananas
1 (12-ounce) can natural ginger ale
¼ cup fresh mint leaves, minced, or a couple
    of drops of mint extract
½ cup ice

Blend all the ingredients well, and serve in a tall,
chilled glass garnished with a fresh sprig of mint.

Per serving: Calories 215, Protein 2 g, Fat 1 g,
Carbohydrates 55 g, Fiber 3 g, Calcium 55 mg, Sodium 10 mg

Lemon-Peppermint
SMOOTHIE

*2*servings

Another good summer smoothie, light and refreshing. Try some of the variations as well.

1 cup lemon sorbet
1 cup strong peppermint or spearmint tea
1 cup frozen apple juice concentrate

Place all the ingredients in the blender, and blend until smooth.

Per serving: Calories 353, Protein 1 g,
Fat 1 g, Carbohydrates 89 g,
Fiber 1 g, Calcium 28 mg, Sodium 40 mg

VARIATIONS

Substitute lime, orange, or peach sorbet for lemon.

Substitute another tea (chamomile, hibiscus, etc.) for all or part of the mint.

Substitute dairy or dairy-free milk, yogurt, or frozen dessert for the frozen apple juice concentrate.

Raspberry-Orange
JUBILATION

2 servings

Please try young coconuts if they're available in your area, otherwise you may substitute one 15-ounce can of coconut milk.

> **Juice from 3 Valencia oranges (fresh squeezed)**
> **½ cup frozen mango**
> **¼ cup (or more) frozen raspberries**
> **1 young coconut, water and meat**
> **1 vanilla bean**

Place all the ingredients in a blender, and blend well until smooth. Garnish with an orange slice and a sprig of fresh mint. Serve and enjoy.

Per serving: Calories 325, Protein 4 g,
Fat 21 g, Carbohydrates 36 g,
Fiber 8 g, Calcium 93 mg, Sodium 3 mg

VARIATIONS

Substitute 1½ cups soy, rice, goat, or almond milk, or yogurt for the coconut.

Try ½ teaspoon vanilla extract in place of the vanilla bean.

Substitute fresh pineapple juice for the orange juice.

Add a scoop of vanilla ice cream or orange (or raspberry) sherbet, for a special treat.

Exotic
SMOOTHIES
from distant lands

Almond-Ginger
SMOOTHIE

2 servings

This refreshing smoothie will delight young and old alike with the zesty flavor of ginger spicing up the smooth richness of the almonds. Freeze some in ice cube trays, and serve in glasses of apple juice for a delightful summer treat.

> **1 cup almonds**
> **1½ cups apple juice**
> **1 cup distilled water,**
>   **or 2 cups almond milk**
> **2 tablespoons raw honey or brown rice syrup**
> **¼ cup ginger juice***
> **½ cup ice (optional)**

Soak the almonds in the apple juice for two days, then blend with the distilled water. Add the honey or brown rice syrup, ginger juice, and ice, and blend well. Serve and enjoy!

Per serving: Calories 510, Protein 15 g,
Fat 40 g, Carbohydrates 33 g,
Fiber 8 g, Calcium 203 mg, Sodium 9 mg

VARIATIONS

For an extra nutritional boost, add 2 tablespoons protein powder, or 1 teaspoon bee pollen, flaxseed oil, or spirulina.

If you like, add a few slices of peaches or pears for an interesting, fruity flavor.

***NOTE:** To make ginger juice, simply grate fresh unpeeled ginger root on a small hand grater. Place the grated pulp in your hand and squeeze. You'll be amazed how much juice you can get this way, without the peel or the pulp!

SweetDateSHAKE

*2*servings

Use Medjool or honey dates from the natural food market rather than those dried dates you find in the produce department of the supermarket around the holidays. This surprisingly rich, sweet shake makes a great holiday smoothie, sort of like a rich eggnog without the egg.

> **12 large dates, pitted**
> **½ cup raw cashews**
> **½ cup distilled water**
> **Dash of pure vanilla**
> **½ teaspoon ground cinnamon**
> **Pinch of nutmeg**

Blend all the ingredients together well. Garnish with a cinnamon stick in a tall, chilled glass. Enjoy!

Per serving: Calories 354, Protein 7 g,
Fat 18 g, Carbohydrates 49 g,
Fiber 5 g, Calcium 33 mg, Sodium 8 mg

VARIATIONS

Substitute apple juice or orange juice for the distilled water.

Rainbow'sEnd
SMOOTHIE

Sweet and spicy, this golden smoothie is a real treasure. Blend the ingredients and serve in a frosted glass with an orange twist.

- **½ cup strongly brewed chai tea**
- **1 mango, peeled and seeded, or soaked dried mango (see page 32)**
- **1 scoop orange or peach sorbet**
- **1 cup orange juice**

Per serving: Calories 178, Protein 2 g,
Fat 1 g, Carbohydrates 44 g,
Fiber 3 g, Calcium 25 mg, Sodium 8 mg

JasmineApple
SMOOTHIE

The sensuous flavor of jasmine tea with sweet apple juice—what a delightful combination! Sip this slowly and savor the moment. If you like, you can substitute your favorite herbal or exotic tea—hibiscus, red zinger, mint, or green tea all work well, or try it with yerba maté.

- **1 cup very strong jasmine tea**
- **2 cups frozen apple juice concentrate**
- **1 tablespoon lemon juice (optional)**

Blend well. Serve in a tall, chilled glass garnished with a slice of lemon.

Per serving: Calories 467, Protein 1 g,
Fat 1 g, Carbohydrates 115 g,
Fiber 1 g, Calcium 56 mg, Sodium 70 mg

JadeDynasty
CucumberWHIP

2 servings

Cucumbers may seem an odd choice for a smoothie, but this refreshing drink will have you coming back for seconds. After all, a cucumber is actually a fruit, and not all that far removed from a watermelon. In fact, don't tell your family and see if anyone can guess what is in this.

2 cucumbers, peeled and seeded
1 cup frozen apple juice concentrate
1 cup lemon sorbet
¼ cup chopped mint leaves

Place all ingredients in the blender, and blend well.
Serve in a tall glass with a fresh sprig of mint. Enjoy!

Per serving: Calories 392, Protein 3 g,
Fat 1 g, Carbohydrates 97 g,
Fiber 4 g, Calcium 70 mg, Sodium 46 mg

VARIATIONS

Add ½ cup strong jasmine, green, or red zinger herbal tea.
Add just a tiny pinch of cardamom.

ThaiGinger-Pineapple
SMOOTHIE

2 servings

This delicious smoothie will take you to foreign ports without leaving home. Blend well and enjoy!

2 cups fresh or frozen pineapple
1 cup frozen orange juice concentrate
1 tablespoon ginger juice*

Per serving: Calories 301, Protein 4 g,
Fat 1 g, Carbohydrates 73 g,
Fiber 3 g, Calcium 56 mg, Sodium 6 mg

VARIATIONS

Substitute frozen apple juice concentrate for the pineapple or frozen orange juice concentrate

Add a scoop of frozen dessert or yogurt, if desired.

*****NOTE:** To make ginger juice, simply grate fresh unpeeled ginger root on a small hand grater. Place the grated pulp in your hand and squeeze. You'll be amazed how much juice you can get this way, without the peel or the pulp!

MoroccanDelight
SMOOTHIE

2 servings

This unusual smoothie makes a great accompaniment to a meal or an after-workout refresher.

> **2 cups orange juice**
> **1 cup chopped carrots**
> **2 tablespoons lemon juice**
> **Pinch of cardamom or ginger**
> **1 cup ice**
> **2 tablespoons honey (optional)**

Place all ingredients together in the blender, and blend well until the carrot is finely chopped.

Per serving: Calories 139, Protein 2 g, Fat 1 g,
Carbohydrates 33 g, Fiber 2 g, Calcium 43 mg, Sodium 22 mg

MoroccanOrange
SMOOTHIE

2 servings

Sip this exotic smoothie slowly, with your eyes closed, and see if you can feel a cool desert breeze. High in protein with a delightful sesame richness, this makes a good meal-in-a-blender. Blend the ingredients well, and serve in a frosted glass garnished with an orange twist.

> **½ cup sesame tahini**
> **1 cup frozen orange juice concentrate or brown rice syrup**
> **1 cup ice**
> **1 cup amazake**
> **2 tablespoons honey or brown rice syrup**

Per serving: Calories 660, Protein 15 g, Fat 29 g,
Carbohydrates 94 g, Fiber 7 g, Calcium 299 mg, Sodium 51 mg

Savory Coconut-Mint
LASSI

2 servings

Lassi is a very popular and refreshing yogurt drink in its native India and Pakistan. This will be popular with your family as well.

1 (15-ounce) can coconut milk
1 cup dairy or dairy-free vanilla or plain yogurt
¼ cup minced fresh mint leaves
1 cup ice
2 teaspoons honey or brown rice syrup (optional)
¼ cup shredded coconut, toasted slightly (for garnish)

Place all the ingredients except the shredded coconut into the blender, and mix well. Serve in a tall, chilled glass, garnished with the coconut, and enjoy.

Per serving: Calories 611, Protein 11 g,
Fat 55 g, Carbohydrates 28 g,
Fiber 5 g, Calcium 253 mg, Sodium 114 mg

AlmondLASSI

This delightfully nutty smoothie uses soaked almonds. The soaking helps the digestibility and releases the enzymes found in raw almonds. The resulting flavor is wonderful!

> **1 cup raw almonds**
> **1 cup distilled or spring water**
> **1 cup raw, unfiltered apple juice**
> **1 cup ice**
> **2 tablespoons honey or maple syrup (optional)**
> **Pinch of cinnamon, cardamom, or nutmeg**

Soak the almonds for 48 hours in the cup of distilled or spring water. Add the rest of the ingredients, blend well, and serve in a chilled glass garnished with a cinnamon stick. Enjoy!

Per serving: Calories 504, Protein 15 g,
Fat 40 g, Carbohydrates 30 g,
Fiber 8 g, Calcium 210 mg, Sodium 12 mg

Spicy LASSI

In India, lassis are often redolent with spices and chiles. If you're a fellow chile-head, you'll love this. Cool and hot at the same time!

> **2 cups dairy or dairy-free plain yogurt**
> **½ cup cilantro (fresh coriander), minced**
> **⅛ teaspoon ground cumin**
> **1 teaspoon fresh ginger juice***
> **1 cup ice**
> **2 teaspoons honey or brown rice syrup (optional)**
> **Fresh or dried chile peppers to taste**

Blend ingredients well until smooth and light green, and serve immediately in a frosted glass. Enjoy!

Per serving: Calories 160, Protein 13 g,
Fat 4 g, Carbohydrates 18 g,
Fiber .1 g, Calcium 462 mg, Sodium 177 mg

***NOTE:** To make ginger juice, simply grate fresh unpeeled ginger root on a small hand grater. Place the grated pulp in your hand and squeeze. You'll be amazed how much juice you can get this way, without the peel or the pulp!

MangoLASSI

This delightful mango smoothie is one of the best of many good reasons to patronize your local Indian restaurants.

Now you can easily make and enjoy this sweet, refreshing drink at home whenever you like. (But do continue to enjoy Indian restaurants for all the other good reasons.)

2 mangoes, peeled and seeded
2 cups dairy or dairy-free yogurt
2 tablespoons raw honey or dehydrated cane juice sweetener
1 teaspoon rose water or juice of 1 lime (optional)
½ cup ice (optional)

Blend everything together well and serve, chilled, in a tall glass. Garnish with a fresh mint leaf and enjoy!

Per serving: Calories 357, Protein 14 g,
Fat 4 g, Carbohydrates 70 g,
Fiber 4 g, Calcium 480 mg, Sodium 181 mg

VARIATIONS

Add a small pinch of cardamom or cinnamon.

Substitute buttermilk or kefir for the yogurt.

Substitute stewed or hydrated dried mangoes for fresh mangoes (see page 32).

Southwest SMOOTHIE

2 servings

OK, I admit we're stretching it a bit here—the Southwest is not actually a distant land, but it does provide some very different and exotic flavors. You may need to order prickly pear syrup through a mail order or Internet source, but trust me, it's worth it. This delicious smoothie will have you shouting "yippee-i-ki-yay" like an old ranch hand.

1 cup frozen orange juice concentrate
1 cup frozen mango
2 tablespoons prickly pear syrup
2 frozen bananas
Juice of 2 limes

Place all the ingredients in the blender, and blend until smooth and creamy. Enjoy!

Per serving: Calories 497, Protein 6 g,
Fat 2 g, Carbohydrates 125 g,
Fiber 9 g, Calcium 80 mg, Sodium 10 mg

VARIATIONS

Substitute pineapple or apple juice for the orange juice.

If fresh mangoes are available, substitute them for the frozen mangoes.

ArizonaHeatwave
SMOOTHIE

2 servings

Here's another one of those exotic flavors that you might not expect to find in a smoothie. I just love this one, hot and cold in the same taste! Wow! If you're not a chile-head, substitute a little mild chili powder for the fresh chiles.

1 cup frozen mango
1 cup frozen pineapple
2 frozen bananas
1 cup raw, unfiltered apple juice
1 fresh chile, your choice of heat, seeded and minced
1 teaspoon lime juice

Blend all the ingredients together well, and serve in a tall frosted mug with a spoon. Enjoy!

Per serving: Calories 255, Protein 2 g,
Fat 1 g, Carbohydrates 65 g,
Fiber 6 g, Calcium 29 mg, Sodium 7 mg

Coronado's
GOLDENDREAM

2 servings

If Coronado had been more observant, he would have noticed the abundant treasure of tropical fruits in the jungles around him (alright, he wouldn't have seen kiwis, but the rest, anyway) and settled down and forgotten the lost cities of gold. However, you can savor the rich tropical sweetness anytime you like.

2 kiwis
1 banana, fresh or frozen
½ cup orange juice
½ cup frozen mango
½ cup ice (optional)

Peel and chop the kiwis. Place all the ingredients in your blender, and blend until smooth. Pour into a tall glass and garnish with a kiwi slice and a sprig of fresh mint, perhaps. Enjoy!

Per serving: Calories 154, Protein 2 g,
Fat 1 g, Carbohydrates 38 g,
Fiber 5 g, Calcium 34 mg, Sodium 6 mg

VARIATIONS

When frozen or fresh mangoes are not available, substitute chopped dried mango soaked in water for 20 minutes (see page 32). You can use scissors to chop the mango.

You might like to substitute fresh or frozen papaya or pineapple for the mango, or mango or pineapple juice for the orange juice. You can also substitute frozen juice concentrate for either.

Tropical fruit sherbet (orange, pineapple, etc.) would make this a wonderful dessert smoothie.

Dairy & Nondairy
Milk-based
Smoothies
&Frappés

SonoranCinnamon
SILENCE

The silence comes from being so busy savoring this rich, spicy treat that you forget to talk! For a decadent dessert, try it with dairy or dairy-free frozen dessert in place of the yogurt.

> **3 frozen bananas**
> **1 cup raw, unfiltered apple juice**
> **1 cup dairy or dairy-free yogurt**
> **¼ teaspoon pure vanilla**
> **1 teaspoon ground cinnamon**

Blend together the bananas, apple juice, yogurt, vanilla, and ground cinnamon until smooth. Serve garnished with cinnamon sticks and dairy or dairy-free whipped cream. Enjoy!

Per serving: Calories 295, Protein 8 g,
Fat 3 g, Carbohydrates 63 g,
Fiber 4 g, Calcium 248 mg, Sodium 94 mg

Pear WHIP

This is refreshing and light, perfect for a hot summer day! Add a pinch of cardamom for an unusual and exciting flavor.

- **4 very ripe pears**
- **1 cup raw, unfiltered apple juice**
- **2 tablespoons lemon juice**
- **1 cup dairy or dairy-free yogurt**
- **4 ice cubes**
- **2 strawberries (for garnish)**

Whip together the pears, apple juice, lemon juice, yogurt, and ice cubes in the blender until smooth and frothy. Garnish with a fresh strawberry.

Per serving: Calories 337, Protein 8 g, Fat 3 g, Carbohydrates 75 g, Fiber 9 g, Calcium 275 mg, Sodium 92 mg

Banana-Cappuccino
FROTH

2 servings

Use either coffee or a grain beverage and enjoy!

- **2 frozen bananas**
- **1 cup dairy or dairy-free yogurt**
- **1 cup brewed coffee (regular or decaf) or grain beverage, cooled**
- **2 tablespoons raw honey or brown rice syrup**
- **¼ cup crushed ice (optional)**

Blend all the ingredients together well and serve in a tall, frosted glass with a dollop of dairy or dairy-free whipped cream. Enjoy!

Per serving: Calories 251, Protein 8 g, Fat 2 g, Carbohydrates 53 g, Fiber 28 g, Calcium 239 mg, Sodium 92 mg

KeyLimeWHIP

2 servings

This rich drink is so refreshing on a hot summer day. Just lie back on a hammock in the shade and while away the lazy moments sipping and savoring. Forget the yard work. Forget the chores.

1 (12.3-ounce) package soft silken tofu
1¼ cups dairy or dairy-free milk (or fresh coconut milk)
6 tablespoons lime juice
6 tablespoons dehydrated sugar cane juice granules
Dash of pure vanilla (optional)

Whip all ingredients together well in a blender, and serve in a tall, frosted glass. Garnish with a lime twist and a sprig of fresh mint.

Per serving: Calories 333, Protein 17 g,
Fat 8 g, Carbohydrates 52 g,
Fiber 2 g, Calcium 239 mg, Sodium 135 mg

TropicalStrawberry
SMOOTHIE

2 servings

An interesting mix of strawberries and tropical flavors, sort of the best of both worlds. Celebrate cultural diversity!

1 cup frozen strawberries
1 cup frozen pineapple juice concentrate
1 kiwi, peeled and chopped
2 frozen bananas
1 cup coconut milk

Blend all ingredients together and serve.

Per serving: Calories 644, Protein 6 g,
Fat 27 g, Carbohydrates 105 g,
Fiber 9 g, Calcium 105 mg, Sodium 24 mg

SmoothiePOWER

OrangeAlmondJOY

2 servings

This interesting smoothie is chock full of nutrition, but it tastes just sinfully delicious. This is one of my favorites.

½ cup almonds, soaked in enough water to cover for 2 days
1 cup fresh orange juice
1 cup fresh coconut milk (or canned if fresh is not available)
1 teaspoon vanilla extract
¼ cup young coconut meat (optional)

Blend all ingredients together well and serve.
Garnish with an orange twist. Enjoy!

Per serving: Calories 515, Protein 11 g,
Fat 46 g, Carbohydrates 24 g,
Fiber 7 g, Calcium 136 mg, Sodium 21 mg

VARIATIONS

For a stronger orange flavor, substitute frozen orange juice concentrate for the fresh orange juice.

Substitute rice or soymilk for the coconut milk.

Cran-Raspberry Whip

3 servings

This beautiful, rich smoothie makes a refreshing dessert. If you wish to avoid the seeds from the raspberries, line a large strainer with cheesecloth, and mash the berries, letting the juice run through into a bowl or glass. You might also try frozen raspberry juice concentrate.

1 (12-ounce) can fruit-sweetened cranberry sauce

1⅓ cups frozen raspberries, or 1 cup fresh raspberries and ½ cup ice

1 (12.3-ounce) package soft silken tofu

3 tablespoons honey or maple syrup

⅔ cup raspberry sorbet or frozen apple juice concentrate

Blend everything well and serve. Enjoy!

Per serving: Calories 392, Protein 8 g,
Fat 3 g, Carbohydrates 84 g,
Fiber 7 g, Calcium 49 mg, Sodium 97 mg

VARIATIONS

Substitute frozen strawberries or blueberries for the raspberries.

Serve this as a topping over cheesecake or pound cake.

Apricot-BananaFRAPPÉ

2 servings

I never thought I cared for apricots until I tasted some ripe and falling from the tree. Though I still don't care for dried or canned apricots, fresh apricots are one of my favorite fruits. They blend especially well with peaches and bananas, as you'll find in this flavorful drink.

4 to 6 fresh apricots, pitted, peeled or unpeeled
2 frozen bananas
1 cup dairy or dairy-free vanilla yogurt
1 cup apple juice
1 tablespoon wheat germ
1 cup ice (if using fresh fruit)

Blend everything together well until smooth and frothy. Serve and enjoy!

Per serving: Calories 323, Protein 9 g,
Fat 3 g, Carbohydrates 70 g,
Fiber 6 g, Calcium 238 mg, Sodium 87 mg

VARIATIONS

Substitute peaches for the apricots.

Substitute apricot or peach sorbet for the yogurt, and add ½ teaspoon vanilla.

Cantaloupe-Melon
COOLER

2 servings

A wonderful way to cool off on a hot summer afternoon. And what a punch of potassium, calcium, vitamin C, and beta-carotene! Serve in a frosted mug, perhaps, for extra cooling power!

1 cup frozen cantaloupe
1 cup frozen watermelon
1 cup frozen orange juice concentrate
1 cup dairy or dairy-free milk

Blend all the ingredients together well until smooth. Serve in a tall glass with a sprig of mint and a slice of orange. Enjoy!

Per serving: Calories 340, Protein 9 g,
Fat 3 g, Carbohydrates 72 g,
Fiber 2 g, Calcium 209 mg, Sodium 74 mg

VARIATIONS

Substitute honeydew or other melon for the cantaloupe or the watermelon.

Substitute apple juice for the milk.

Add a tablespoon of fresh mint to the blender.

Yam-Orange
SMOOTHIE

2 servings

This unusual smoothie is so flavorful (and colorful) you'll want to enjoy it often. Very rich and filling, this makes a good replacement for a meal, also.

1 large baked yam or sweet potato, peeled and chopped
1 cup frozen orange juice concentrate
¾ cup dairy or dairy-free milk or yogurt
2 tablespoons honey or maple syrup (optional)
½ cup ice (optional)

Blend all the ingredients together well, and serve garnished with a cinnamon stick. Enjoy!

Per serving: Calories 329, Protein 7 g,
Fat 2 g, Carbohydrates 72 g,
Fiber 3 g, Calcium 173 mg, Sodium 56 mg

VARIATIONS

Add a pinch of pumpkin pie spices (cinnamon, nutmeg, allspice, and cloves).

Substitute soft silken tofu for the milk or yogurt.

Rice-Coconut FRAPPÉ

2 servings

Amazake is a sweet rice drink found in most natural food stores and co-ops. Delicious and very healthy, it makes a wonderful base for this delicious tropical smoothie.

2 cups of your favorite flavor amazake
1 cup fresh or canned coconut milk
½ cup ice

Whip all the ingredients well in a blender until thick and creamy. Serve and enjoy!

Per serving: Calories 291, Protein 4 g,
Fat 26 g, Carbohydrates 15 g,
Fiber 3 g, Calcium 26 mg, Sodium 18 mg

VARIATIONS

Substitute pineapple-coconut juice (or other juice) for the coconut milk.

Add just a dash of vanilla.

Peachy Buttermilk
FRAPPÉ

2 servings

Buttermilk is generally a low-fat dairy food with a healthful bacteria culture, somewhat like yogurt. It has a distinctive sour flavor similar to yogurt as well. The buttermilk and cottage cheese in this recipe add a rich creaminess you are sure to enjoy. If you are avoiding dairy products, try this with soy yogurt or amazake.

> **1 cup frozen peaches**
> **½ cup frozen apple juice concentrate**
> **1 cup 1% buttermilk plus ½ cup 1% cottage cheese,**
> **or 1½ cups soy yogurt or amazake**

Blend all ingredients well and enjoy!

Per serving: Calories 325, Protein 12 g,
Fat 2 g, Carbohydrates 66 g,
Fiber 2 g, Calcium 195 mg, Sodium 383 mg

VARIATIONS

Substitute frozen orange or orange-mango juice concentrate for the frozen apple juice concentrate.

Try frozen apricots in place of the peaches.

Add a pinch of ground ginger or cinnamon, if you like.

PapayaCreamsicle
SMOOTHIE

2 servings

This refreshing smoothie is rich in papain, a digestive enzyme. So, though it may taste sinfully delicious, you're really doing your body a favor by enjoying this cooler.

1 large papaya, peeled, seeded, and chopped
½ cup papaya juice concentrate
1 cup vanilla dairy or dairy-free frozen dessert or yogurt
½ teaspoon vanilla
1 teaspoon lime juice
2 tablespoons honey or maple syrup (optional)

Blend all the ingredients together well. Serve and enjoy!

Per serving: Calories 242, Protein 4 g,
Fat 8 g, Carbohydrates 38 g,
Fiber 3 g, Calcium 140 mg, Sodium 51 mg

VARIATIONS

Substitute frozen orange juice concentrate for the papaya concentrate.

Substitute dairy or dairy-free milk or yogurt for the frozen dessert, and add ice cubes.

PeachChaiSMOOTHIE

2 servings

Simple and only slightly spicy, this makes a great autumn or winter smoothie. Kefir is a wonderful cultured milk (like liquid yogurt) and is available in any natural food store or co-op. If you can't find kefir, substitute your favorite yogurt. Pineapple and other flavors also work well.

2 cups prepared, cooled chai tea
1 cup peach kefir
1 cup frozen apple or peach juice concentrate

Blend all the ingredients well and enjoy!

Per serving: Calories 361, Protein 5 g,
Fat 1 g, Carbohydrates 82 g,
Fiber .6 g, Calcium 164 mg, Sodium 97 mg

Triple-ASMOOTHIE

2 servings

No, this smoothie has nothing to do with automobile travel; the name comes from the three main ingredients: apples, avocados, and almond milk. This smooth treat is packed with nutrition and flavor.

1 large or 2 small avocados, peeled and seeded
1 apple, cored and chopped, peeled or unpeeled
1 cup almond milk
1 cup frozen apple juice concentrate
½ cup ice
Pinch of cinnamon, nutmeg, or cardamom (optional)

Blend all ingredients well and serve in a chilled glass. Enjoy!

Per serving: Calories 528, Protein 6 g,
Fat 22 g, Carbohydrates 84 g,
Fiber 7 g, Calcium 85 mg, Sodium 44 mg

MidnightSnack
SMOOTHIE

2 servings

Here's a quick, nutritious snack for when you wake up in the middle of the night with a hollow feeling in your tummy.

> **1 (12.3-ounce) package soft silken tofu**
> **⅔ cup fresh fruit**
> **⅔ cup frozen apple or orange juice concentrate**
> **1 frozen banana**
> **1 teaspoon wheat germ**

Blend the ingredients well and sip slowly. Relax.
Think sleepy thoughts.

Per serving: Calories 316, Protein 10 g,
Fat 6 g, Carbohydrates 59 g,
Fiber 4 g, Calcium 77 mg, Sodium 36 mg

VARIATIONS
You just might add ½ cup strong chamomile tea. The flavor is a nice complement to the fruit, and chamomile has long been valued for its ability to help the body relax.

Peppermint-Coconut-Carrot FRAPPÉ

2 servings

Though it may seem like an unusual combination, this trio of flavors works surprisingly well. Have fun and be bold when looking through your cupboards for smoothie ingredients. Above all, don't be afraid to experiment. If you don't like the result, do something different next time. Be aware of the flavors you do and don't like. Remember: in the kitchen you are omnipotent!

1 cup fresh carrot juice
1 (15-ounce) can of coconut milk,
  or I cup fresh coconut milk
1 cup strong peppermint tea
1 cup ice (optional)

Place all ingredients in the blender, and process until smooth. Serve and enjoy, garnished with a sprig of peppermint.

Per serving: Calories 492, Protein 6 g,
Fat 48 g, Carbohydrates 18 g,
Fiber 6 g, Calcium 70 mg, Sodium 65 mg

Cashew-Vanilla
SMOOTHIE

2 servings

Blending cashews with water until thick creates a wonderful milk substitute, sort of a cashew milk. This nutty smoothie is sure to please, and the fresh vanilla beans and maple syrup add just the right amount of flavor.

> **1 cup raw cashews**
> **1 cup water**
> **2 tablespoons pure maple syrup**
> **2 vanilla beans cut into ¼-inch pieces**
> **½ cup ice**

Blend all ingredients together until very smooth.
Serve in a frosted glass and enjoy!

Per serving: Calories 487, Protein 12 g,
Fat 35 g, Carbohydrates 38 g,
Fiber 2 g, Calcium 47 mg, Sodium 14 mg

VARIATIONS

Try this with almonds, but soak the almonds for 48 hours to make them softer and easier to digest.

Add a pinch of cinnamon or nutmeg, if you like.

AthleticBoosters &Healing SMOOTHIES

Runner'sHighProtein
POWERSURGE

2 servings

This nutrient-dense power shake will give you the energy for that long run or intense workout! Sip slowly and feel the energy building up.

> 1 cup vanilla soy or rice milk
> 2 frozen bananas
> ¼ cup wheat germ
> 1 tablespoon flaxseed oil
> ¼ cup raw pecans
> 2 tablespoons protein powder
> ½ cup frozen apple juice concentrate
> 1 teaspoon carob-mint spirulina powder (optional)

Blend together well and serve. Enjoy!

Per serving: Calories 482, Protein 12 g,
Fat 21 g, Carbohydrates 69 g,
Fiber 8 g, Calcium 52 mg, Sodium 35 mg

VARIATIONS
Add other fresh or frozen fruit as desired.

Substitute dairy or dairy-free yogurt for the soy or rice milk.

HighC's SMOOTHIE

2 servings

Linus Pauling, who discovered the power of vitamin C, would have loved this wonderful smoothie. You will too! Blend all the ingredients until smooth. Serve immediately and enjoy.

> **1 cup fresh orange juice**
> **1 cup fresh pineapple juice**
> **1 cup carrot juice**
> **2 kiwis, peeling optional**
> **1 sweet red bell pepper, seeded and chopped**
> **1 teaspoon vitamin C powder (optional)**

Per serving: Calories 221, Protein 4 g,
Fat 1 g, Carbohydrates 53 g,
Fiber 5 g, Calcium 76 mg, Sodium 46 mg

Figgy-Flax FRAPPÉ

2 servings

Enjoy this soothing smoothie whenever you're feeling a little "irregular," as they say. Medicine just never tasted so good.

> **6 figs, stewed or soaked**
> **2 frozen bananas**
> **3 cups apple juice**
> **1 tablespoon psyllium seed husks**
> **2 teaspoons flaxseed oil**
> **½ cup ice (optional)**

Process everything together in the blender until smooth. Enjoy!

Per serving: Calories 472, Protein 3 g,
Fat 6 g, Carbohydrates 109 g,
Fiber 9 g, Calcium 119 mg, Sodium 19 mg

SunflowerSeed-OatBranSMOOTHIE

2 servings

Here's a really tasty high-fiber, high-protein smoothie. Freeze it the night before and take it with you for a quick mid-morning energy drink or simple lunch.

1 cup oat or almond milk
1 cup raw, unfiltered apple juice
2 frozen bananas
¼ cup sunflower seeds
¼ cup oat bran
2 tablespoons honey or maple syrup
2 tablespoons wheat germ
2 tablespoons protein powder
1 or 2 tablespoons flaxseeds or oil
1 teaspoon vanilla or other flavoring
¼ cup stewed raisins or pitted prunes (optional)
2 teaspoons spirulina (optional)
2 teaspoons bee pollen (optional)

Place all the ingredients together in the blender container, and blend until smooth. Enjoy!

Per serving: Calories 533, Protein 13 g,
Fat 22 g, Carbohydrates 82 g,
Fiber 9 g, Calcium 69 mg, Sodium 8 mg

VARIATIONS

Add other frozen fruit, substitute another juice, add or omit nutritional ingredients as you desire.

Add carob or cocoa powder, chopped pecans or hazelnuts, carob or chocolate chips.

MegaSMOOTHIE

2 servings

This thick, creamy smoothie has it all—mega flavor and mega nutrition. What a great way to begin your day, or a refreshing pick-me-up after a workout.

> **1 mango, peeled, seeded, and chopped**
> **2 frozen bananas**
> **½ cup frozen strawberries**
> **1 cup fresh carrot juice**
> **1 cup dairy or dairy-free yogurt or buttermilk**
> **2 tablespoons wheat germ**
> **1 cup ice**
> **2 tablespoons honey or maple syrup (optional)**
> **2 tablespoons carob-mint spirulina (optional)**
> **2 tablespoons flaxseeds or oil (optional)**

Blend all ingredients well and pour into a large, chilled glass.

Per serving: Calories 338, Protein 11 g, Fat 4 g, Carbohydrates 71 g, Fiber 8 g, Calcium 284 mg, Sodium 128 mg

VARIATIONS

If fresh mango is unavailable, simply soak dried mango for about 20 minutes in warm water to soften and hydrate it (see page 32).

Substitute, perhaps, fresh or frozen pineapple for the mango.

Add, if you desire, some fresh coconut milk or coconut-pineapple juice, or orange-mango juice.

Carob-MintSpirulina
SMOOTHIE

2 servings

Carob and mint are often added to spirulina to help cover up the seaweed flavor. This tasty smoothie adds even more carob and mint just to make it delicious. What a good way to add a little spirulina into your diet!

2 cups dairy or dairy-free milk or yogurt
1 cup ice or frozen apple juice concentrate
1 tablespoon carob powder
Fresh mint leaves
2 tablespoons carob-mint flavored spirulina
1 tablespoon honey or dehydrated sugar cane juice granules

Place all the ingredients in a blender, and blend until smooth and creamy. Serve and enjoy!

Per serving: Calories 167, Protein 8 g,
Fat 5 g, Carbohydrates 24 g,
Fiber .6 g, Calcium 307 mg, Sodium 123 mg

VARIATIONS

Substitute ice cream or frozen yogurt for the milk.

Substitute cocoa powder for the carob powder.

For a mocha flavor, add 1 tablespoon instant coffee or grain beverage.

Tummy-Soothing
SMOOTHIE

2 servings

This refreshing drink is wonderful for coating and healing the stomach lining. It sure doesn't taste like medicine, though! Blend all the ingredients well and serve.

2 fresh kiwis, peeling optional
1 cup frozen cantaloupe
2 frozen bananas
¼ cup fresh mint leaves
⅓ cup frozen apple juice concentrate

Per serving: Calories 256, Protein 3 g,
Fat 1 g, Carbohydrates 64 g,
Fiber 6 g, Calcium 45 mg, Sodium 24 mg

VARIATIONS

Add 1 teaspoon fresh ginger juice*.

Add ½ cup oat milk.

*NOTE: To make ginger juice, simply grate fresh unpeeled ginger root on a small hand grater. Place the grated pulp in your hand and squeeze. You'll be amazed how much juice you can get this way, without the peel or the pulp!

Wheatgrass-Orange Juice SMOOTHIE

2 servings

Fresh wheatgrass is chock full of enzymes and nutrients, but the flavor is often too strong for the uninitiated. The orange juice in this smoothie helps to make the wheatgrass more palatable. Blend the ingredients together well, and serve immediately.

2 ounces fresh wheatgrass juice
3 cups fresh squeezed orange juice
½ cup ice (optional)

Per serving: Calories 167, Protein 3 g,
Fat 1 g, Carbohydrates 39 g,
Fiber 1 g, Calcium 41 mg, Sodium 4 mg

BettyCarotene COOLER

2 servings

High in beta-carotene, this nutritious smoothie tastes too good to be so good for you, but it is! Drink up!

2 cups fresh carrot juice
1 cup frozen orange juice concentrate
2 frozen bananas
1 cup chopped cantaloupe or honeydew melon, seeded and peeled
2 tablespoons honey or maple syrup (optional)

Place all the ingredients into the blender container, and blend well until smooth. Serve in a tall, chilled glass and enjoy!

Per serving: Calories 457, Protein 8 g,
Fat 1 g, Carbohydrates 110 g,
Fiber 7 g, Calcium 120 mg, Sodium 84 mg

Lemon-Ginger-Echinacea
ImmuneBuilder

2 servings

Echinacea has long been a popular treatment for strengthening the immune system. The combination of echinacea with fresh squeezed lemon and ginger juice makes for a pretty powerful smoothie. If you want to give your system an extra kick, add a pinch of cayenne.

1 cup hot water
⅓ cup honey or maple syrup
½ cup fresh squeezed lemon juice
1 tablespoon fresh ginger juice (see notes)
1 cup cold water
Echinacea tincture (follow directions on bottle
   for amount; see notes)
½ cup ice

In a large glass or bowl, combine the hot water and honey to dissolve. Pour this mixture into the blender container with the rest of the ingredients, and blend well. Serve and enjoy!

Per serving: Calories 175, Protein 0 g,
Fat 0 g, Carbohydrates 48 g,
Fiber .3 g, Calcium 7 mg, Sodium 3 mg

NOTES

Some nutritional health care professionals suggest combining goldenseal with echinacea. Check with your health care practitioner before taking any strong medicines and herbal preparations.

To make ginger juice, simply grate fresh unpeeled ginger root on a small hand grater. Place the grated pulp in your hand and squeeze. You'll be amazed how much juice you can get this way, without the peel or the pulp!

Apricot-Ginger
SMOOTHIE

2 servings

The smell of fresh ginger is so refreshing, and fresh ginger is sometimes used as a home remedy for an upset stomach or travel sickness. This delicious smoothie, then, may be just what the doctor ordered.

1 cup fresh apricots, pitted, peeled or unpeeled, or
½ cup dried apricots soaked in ½ cup orange juice
1 cup frozen apple juice concentrate
2 frozen bananas
2 teaspoons fresh ginger juice*

Blend all the ingredients together well and serve.
Enjoy!

Per serving: Calories 375, Protein 3 g,
Fat 1 g, Carbohydrates 93 g,
Fiber 5 g, Calcium 46 mg, Sodium 37 mg

*NOTE: To make ginger juice, simply grate fresh unpeeled ginger root on a small hand grater. Place the grated pulp in your hand and squeeze. You'll be amazed how much juice you can get this way, without the peel or the pulp!

Shakes&Dessert
SMOOTHIES

WilcoxApplePieSHAKE

2 servings

The Southeastern Arizona town of Wilcox is considered by some the "Apple Capital" of the Southwest. When the apple season comes in I like to make these nurturing shakes for a quick dessert. Serve with cookies or graham crackers, perhaps.

> **2 large apples, cored, peeled or not**
> **1 cup dairy or dairy-free yogurt**
> **1 cup dairy or dairy-free milk**
> **2 tablespoons raw honey or maple syrup**
> **1 teaspoon cinnamon**
> **Pinch of nutmeg**
> **Pinch of cloves**

Blend until smooth. Pour into tall glasses and garnish with a cinnamon stick and, if desired, a dollop of vegan or dairy whipped cream. Serve and enjoy!

Per serving: Calories 285, Protein 11 g,
Fat 5 g, Carbohydrates 53 g,
Fiber 4 g, Calcium 388 mg, Sodium 150 mg

VARIATIONS

Substitute frozen yogurt or other frozen dessert for the yogurt.

Substitute granulated cane juice crystals for the honey.

Sprinkle the top lightly with graham cracker crumbs just before serving.

For extra nutrition, if desired, you might add 1 tablespoon protein powder or 1 teaspoon bee pollen.

Cookies&Cream SHAKE

2 servings

Rich and smooth, a delight for the inner child! Reward yourself for something! Anything! Blend well and serve in a tall glass.

4 or 5 of your favorite cookies
2 frozen bananas
2 scoops dairy or dairy-free frozen dessert
1 cup dairy or dairy-free milk

Per serving: Calories 300, Protein 8 g,
Fat 9 g, Carbohydrates 48 g, Fiber 3 g,
Calcium 230 mg, Sodium 125 mg

Oatmeal Cookie SHAKE

2 servings

Here's a tasty way to get your fiber without sacrificing rich, sweet flavor. The prunes taste like raisins. The molasses adds iron and calcium but is pretty strong flavored. Use it only to taste. Blend all the ingredients together well and serve. Enjoy!

¼ cup pitted prunes, soaked in distilled water until soft
¼ cup quick oats
2 scoops dairy or dairy-free yogurt or frozen dessert
1 cup dairy or dairy-free milk
2 tablespoons protein powder
2 tablespoons raw honey or maple syrup
1 teaspoon pure vanilla
½ teaspoon blackstrap molasses (optional)

Per serving: Calories 305, Protein 15 g,
Fat 5 g, Carbohydrates 53 g,
Fiber 3 g, Calcium 410 mg, Sodium 151 mg

Old-FashionedIceCream Parlor STRAWBERRY MALT

2 servings

Don't limit yourself to just strawberries with this one. Fresh or frozen blueberries, raspberries, blackberries, etc., are all wonderful. Blend the ingredients well and garnish with a fresh strawberry or a mint leaf and dairy or dairy-free whipped cream.

1 cup fresh or frozen strawberries
2 cups dairy or dairy-free frozen dessert
½ cup powdered skim milk or soymilk
1 heaping tablespoon malt powder

Per serving: Calories 362, Protein 10 g,
Fat 16 g, Carbohydrates 43 g,
Fiber 3 g, Calcium 321 mg, Sodium 131 mg

Blueberry BUBBLE

2 servings

This dark, rich smoothie tastes every bit as decadent as it looks. Serve in a tall glass with dairy or dairy-free whipped cream.

1 cup fresh or frozen blueberries
1 cup dairy or dairy-free frozen dessert
½ cup honey or maple syrup
2 tablespoons protein powder
¼ cup apple juice
2 frozen bananas (optional)

Blend all the ingredients except the blueberries. Add the blueberries and blend just slightly to leave them somewhat chunky.

Per serving: Calories 475, Protein 6 g,
Fat 8 g, Carbohydrates 99 g, Fiber 3 g,
Calcium 127 mg, Sodium 54 mg

FunkyMonkey
SMOOTHIE

2 servings

This delicious vegan shake packs a lot of nutrition in rich carob/cashew/banana decadence. Try some of the simple variations, also.

> **2 cups soy or rice milk**
>
> **2 ripe bananas**
>
> **4 tablespoons raw or roasted cashews***
>
> **2 tablespoons raw or roasted cocoa or carob powder**
> **plus 2 tablespoons dehydrated sugar cane juice granules, honey, or maple syrup,**
> **or ¼ cup malt-sweetened vegan carob chips or chocolate chips**

In an electric blender, blend all ingredients together until smooth and creamy. Serve garnished with a mint leaf and, perhaps, a dollop of dairy or dairy-free whipped cream. Enjoy!

Per serving: Calories 369, Protein 12 g,
Fat 15 g, Carbohydrates 57 g,
Fiber 8 g, Calcium 33 mg, Sodium 35 mg

VARIATIONS

Add a scoop or two of dairy-free frozen dessert.

Try other fruit (fresh or frozen) in place of the carob—strawberries, raspberries, peaches, etc.

*NOTE: It's very simple to roast raw cashews. Just cook them in a dry, heavy skillet (cast-iron works well) over medium heat, stirring often, until golden brown. These taste better than store-bought, already-roasted cashews.

PeanutButterTwist
SMOOTHIE

2 servings

Sort of a smoothie version of a Reese's Peanut Butter Cup, this is sure to be a favorite with your family and friends! Blend well and serve, garnished with shaved chocolate and roasted peanuts. Share the recipe!

1 cup natural peanut butter
½ cup carob or chocolate chips
1 cup dairy or dairy-free vanilla, carob,
  or chocolate frozen dessert or yogurt
1 cup fresh or canned coconut milk

Per serving: Calories 1,267, Protein 44 g,
Fat 96 g, Carbohydrates 60 g,
Fiber 13 g, Calcium 302 mg, Sodium 364 mg

HazelnutTorte SHAKE

2 servings

I was once served a delicious chocolate-hazelnut torte at a very nice restaurant. I liked it so much I incorporated it into this extravagant dessert smoothie. I hope you enjoy it as well. Blend all the ingredients well, and serve in a chilled glass with a dollop of dairy or dairy-free whipped cream and a spoon. Enjoy!

1 cup dairy or dairy-free frozen dessert or yogurt
1 cup dairy or dairy-free milk or yogurt
1 carob or chocolate brownie, crumbled
¼ cup hazelnuts or filberts

Per serving: Calories 380, Protein 10 g,
Fat 23 g, Carbohydrates 34 g,
Fiber 1 g, Calcium 284 mg, Sodium 151 mg

Kiwi-Lime WHIP

servings

Put the blended smoothie back in the freezer, if desired, for about a half an hour, and serve as a wonderfully refreshing dessert by itself or over cheesecake.

> **2½ kiwis, chopped, peeling optional**
> **6 tablespoons lime juice**
> **2½ tablespoons honey or maple syrup**
> **1 (12.3-ounce) package soft silken tofu**
> **1½ cups frozen apple juice concentrate**
> **1½ frozen bananas**

Place all ingredients in the blender, and blend well until smooth and creamy. Top, if you like, with dairy or dairy-free whipped cream. Garnish with a lime twist. Serve and enjoy!

Per serving: Calories 588, Protein 11 g,
Fat 6 g, Carbohydrates 130 g,
Fiber 7 g, Calcium 118 mg, Sodium 62 mg

VARIATIONS

For the tofu, substitute yogurt, buttermilk, frozen yogurt, or frozen dessert (either dairy or dairy-free).

Substitute frozen pineapple juice concentrate for the apple.

Substitute ricotta cheese for the tofu.

PurpleCow(orBean)
SMOOTHIE

2 servings

Traditionally, a "purple cow" is a Concord grape juice–vanilla ice cream float. Your family will enjoy this beautiful lavender variation. Blend all the ingredients well, and serve in a frosted glass. Enjoy!

1 cup frozen Concord grape juice concentrate
3 cups dairy or dairy-free milk or yogurt
½ cup ice (optional)

Per serving: Calories 439, Protein 13 g, Fat 7 g, Carbohydrates 81 g, Fiber 0 g, Calcium 464 mg, Sodium 193 mg

ButterscotchSHAKE

2 servings

Get out your plaid clothes and prepare to enjoy the wonderful taste of butterscotch in a creamy smooth treat!

2 cups dairy or dairy-free vanilla ice cream
  or frozen dessert or yogurt
1 cup dairy or dairy-free milk, yogurt, or buttermilk
½ teaspoon natural butterscotch or caramel flavoring
1 tablespoon maple or rice syrup, honey, or Barbados
  molasses (optional)

Place all the ingredients into a blender, and blend until smooth and creamy. Serve in a frosted glass with dairy or dairy-free whipped cream and a spoon.

Per serving: Calories 361, Protein 10 g, Fat 18 g, Carbohydrates 36 g, Fiber 0 g, Calcium 348 mg, Sodium 151 mg

TIP: If you can't find natural butterscotch or caramel flavoring, lightly brown 2 tablespoons granulated sugar cane juice in 1 tablespoon butter or oil, and mix with a drop of vanilla.

Maple-PecanTreeHugger
SHAKE

2 servings

Here's a rich, nutty shake that will give you a new appreciation of the sugar maples, pecan trees, and so many others that provide us with wholesome, delicious foods. Imitation maple-flavored syrup could never replace the flavor of pure maple syrup. This makes a wonderful dessert smoothie or party drink, served fresh from the blender.

1 cup vanilla cream natural soda
1 cup dairy or dairy-free frozen dessert in a compatible flavor (vanilla, butter pecan, caramel, etc.)
¼ cup real maple syrup
⅓ cup shelled pecans
1 cup ice

Blend well and serve in a tall, frosted mug, perhaps garnished with a dollop of dairy or vegan whipped cream and a cinnamon stick. Enjoy!

Per serving: Calories 443, Protein 4 g,
Fat 21 g, Carbohydrates 62 g,
Fiber 1 g, Calcium 140 mg, Sodium 267 mg

VARIATIONS

Sometimes I like to add a handful of granola to the blender or sprinkle it on top as a crunchy garnish.

Substitute milk or yogurt (dairy or dairy-free) or coconut milk for the ice cream.

Add a dash of natural butterscotch or caramel flavor.

Substitute walnuts for the pecans.

Add a couple of frozen bananas, if you like.

PumpkinPieSHAKE

2servings

Who says pumpkin pie is just for Thanksgiving? Your family will enjoy this rich treat any time of year. Another wonderful dessert or party shake!

> **1 (15-ounce) can organic pumpkin and ½ cup ice,
>   or 2 cups frozen pumpkin**
> **1 cup dairy or dairy-free vanilla ice cream**
> **Small pinch each of cinnamon, nutmeg, and allspice**
> **Very small pinch of cloves**
> **2 tablespoons honey or maple syrup**

Place all the ingredients in the blender, and blend until smooth and creamy. Serve, perhaps with a dollop of vegan or dairy whipped cream and sprinkled with crushed graham crackers or cookie crumbs. Enjoy!

Per serving: Calories 275, Protein 5 g,
Fat 9 g, Carbohydrates 46 g,
Fiber 6 g, Calcium 169 mg, Sodium 57 mg

VARIATIONS

Add a little applesauce or frozen apple juice concentrate for an interesting flavor.

Add a few raisins (soak them in apple juice until soft).

CoconutCreamPieSHAKE

2 servings

Another sumptuous dessert shake. Why put ice cream on your pie when you can enjoy pie in your ice cream?

1 (12.3-ounce) package soft silken tofu
1½ cups dairy or dairy-free vanilla ice cream or frozen yogurt
6 tablespoons toasted coconut*
1 cup frozen apple or pineapple juice concentrate
2 tablespoons honey or maple syrup (optional)

Blend everything together well and serve. Garnish with graham cracker or cookie crumbs, if desired. Enjoy!

Per serving: Calories 667, Protein 14 g,
Fat 23 g, Carbohydrates 103 g,
Fiber 3 g, Calcium 214 mg, Sodium 118 mg

*TIP: To toast coconut, spread in a small, hot, dry skillet, and lightly stir while toasting, about 5 to 10 minutes or until golden brown and aromatic.

VARIATIONS

Use dairy or dairy-free milk or yogurt in place of the tofu.

Add ½ cup ricotta cheese for a creamy, "cheesecake" flavor.

ArcticForest FRAPPÉ

2 servings

This cool, refreshing smoothie will put you in mind of Northern Lights and warm friends. Share it with someone you care about and smile. Light a fire and cuddle.

1 cup frozen blueberries
1 cup frozen apple juice concentrate
1 cup dairy or dairy-free yogurt or buttermilk
⅓ cup hazelnuts
½ teaspoon vanilla
1 tablespoon carob or cocoa powder (optional)

Place all the ingredients in a blender, and blend until smooth and creamy. Serve, perhaps with a dollop of dairy or vegan whipped cream, and enjoy!

Per serving: Calories 510, Protein 10 g,
Fat 18 g, Carbohydrates 81 g,
Fiber 4 g, Calcium 308 mg, Sodium 128 mg

VARIATIONS

Try pecans in place of the hazelnuts.

Would you prefer raspberries or blackberries instead of blueberries?

BlackForestSHAKE

2 servings

A wonderful way to celebrate any special occasion! Blend all the ingredients until creamy. Top with vegan or dairy whipped cream.

> 1 cup dairy or dairy-free milk or yogurt
> 1 cup frozen dessert or yogurt, vanilla, chocolate, or carob
> ½ cup frozen cherries
> 2 frozen bananas
> 2 tablespoons cocoa or carob powder
> ¼ cup pecans or hazelnuts (optional)

Per serving: Calories 385, Protein 10 g,
Fat 12 g, Carbohydrates 65 g,
Fiber 5 g, Calcium 270 mg, Sodium 109 mg

BananaBlizzardBlast SHAKE

2 servings

Banana, chocolate, and pineapple! Yum! Blend well and serve in a tall, frosted glass. Sprinkle with a few roasted peanuts, or top with a fresh strawberry or cherry and some whipped cream.

> 3 frozen bananas
> 1 cup chopped fresh pineapple
> 2 cups vanilla frozen dessert or yogurt
> 2 tablespoons cocoa or carob powder

Per serving: Calories 508, Protein 9 g,
Fat 18 g, Carbohydrates 83 g,
Fiber 7 g, Calcium 83 mg, Sodium 94 mg

VARIATIONS

Substitute your favorite flavor frozen dessert for the vanilla.

Add a few peanuts or a couple of tablespoons of peanut butter.

Add a dash of vanilla.

DarkCherryFRAPPÉ

This is rich and sinful. Sip it slowly and savor the velvet smoothness of the bananas, the tartness of the cherries, and the decadence of the carob! This is a wonderful dessert for a romantic Valentine's dinner or anniversary.

> **2 cups cherries, pitted (or frozen cherries)**
> **1 frozen banana**
> **1 cup raw, unfiltered apple juice**
> **1 tablespoon carob powder**
> **½ cup ice (optional)**
> **2 cherries with stems (for garnish)**

Blend together the cherries, banana, apple juice, and carob powder until smooth. Serve garnished with cherries. Enjoy!

Per serving: Calories 355, Protein 4 g,
Fat 1 g, Carbohydrates 89 g,
Fiber 5 g, Calcium 53 mg, Sodium 7 mg

VARIATIONS

Add a scoop of dairy or dairy-free frozen dessert.

A tablespoon of protein powder will make it thicker and smoother.

WhiteChocolate-
HazelnutFRAPPÉ

2 servings

As a child I always preferred white chocolate candy to milk or dark chocolate. If you, too, enjoy the smooth, creamy flavor of white chocolate, you'll love this chunky smoothie.

1 cup dairy or dairy-free milk or yogurt
½ cup white chocolate chips or candy, broken into pieces
½ cup hazelnuts
1 cup vanilla frozen dessert or yogurt
Dash of vanilla

Blend all the ingredients well until nuts and chips are fairly well ground. Sprinkle with a couple of white chocolate chips as garnish and enjoy!

Per serving: Calories 706, Protein 15 g,
Fat 50 g, Carbohydrates 51 g,
Fiber 2 g, Calcium 416 mg, Sodium 147mg

VARIATIONS

Add a pinch of cinnamon or nutmeg.

Substitute or add fresh cherries or strawberries.

Chocolate(orCarob)MALT

2 servings

Here's an old favorite with a couple of new ideas. I guess the classics never do go out of style!

> **1 cup dairy or dairy-free milk, regular, chocolate, or carob**
> **2 cups dairy or dairy-free frozen dessert, vanilla, chocolate, or carob**
> **1 heaping tablespoon cocoa or carob powder**
> **1 teaspoon malt powder**

Blend all ingredients well until smooth and creamy. Serve, sprinkled with a few chocolate or carob chips and a dollop of dairy or vegan whipped cream, and enjoy!

Per serving: Calories 367, Protein 11 g,
Fat 19 g, Carbohydrates 37 g,
Fiber 1 g, Calcium 352 mg, Sodium 151 mg

VARIATIONS

Add a few pecans, walnuts, or peanuts.

For an unusual flavor, add cherries or strawberries.

Add 1 tablespoon fresh mint leaves or a couple of drops of mint extract to the blender.

BlackCOW

2 servings

Another old favorite, like a root beer float with the addition of chocolate. This one doesn't need a blender, just two glasses and two spoons. For a different taste, omit the chocolate or carob syrup, or try this with other flavors of natural soda!

2 cups dairy or dairy-free vanilla frozen dessert or yogurt
1 (12-ounce) bottle natural root beer, sarsaparilla, or birch beer
2 tablespoons chocolate or carob syrup

Divide the frozen dessert between two glasses. Add 1 tablespoon chocolate or carob syrup to each glass, and stir just a little to mix, but leave frozen. Pour root beer over the ice cream, and top with a dollop of vegan or dairy whipped cream. Serve with a spoon.

Per serving: Calories 435, Protein 6 g,
Fat 16 g, Carbohydrates 62 g,
Fiber 0 g, Calcium 204 mg, Sodium 114 mg

GoldenSunsetSMOOTHIE

2 servings

This delightful smoothie makes an elegant after-dinner refresher or dessert. If you prefer, you can use sparkling cranberry juice in place of the wine, or frozen raspberries or strawberries for the peaches. Blend all the ingredients well, serve, and enjoy!

1 cup frozen peaches
2 cups blush wine or Zinfandel
½ cup ice

Per serving: Calories 226, Protein 1 g,
Fat 0 g, Carbohydrates 19 g,
Fiber 3 g, Calcium 25 mg, Sodium 12 mg

Maple-ButterPecan
FRAPPÉ

2 servings

So rich and thick, this is one of my favorites. But then, I'm reminded, they're all my favorites. Blend all ingredients well and garnish with a dollop of dairy or vegan whipped cream, a cinnamon stick, and a couple of pecan halves.

> **2 cups dairy or dairy-free butter pecan frozen dessert or yogurt**
> **¼ cup pure maple syrup**
> **1 cup dairy or dairy-free milk or yogurt**
> **1 cup ice**
> **Pinch of cinnamon**

Per serving: Calories 525, Protein 12 g,
Fat 26 g, Carbohydrates 63 g,
Fiber 0 g, Calcium 375 mg, Sodium 314 mg

CandyBarSHAKE

2 servings

You can use any candy bar you like in this recipe, even some of the delicious natural brands. Or try using granola bars—they're surprisingly good! Blend all the ingredients until creamy and smooth, and top with dairy or vegan whipped cream.

> **2 candy bars (your choice), cut into pieces**
> **2 cups frozen dessert or yogurt, vanilla, chocolate, or carob**
> **1 cup dairy or dairy-free milk, vanilla, plain, chocolate, or carob**

Per serving: Calories 561, Protein 14 g,
Fat 30 g, Carbohydrates 57 g,
Fiber 2 g, Calcium 408 mg, Sodium 171 mg

RhubarbCustard
SMOOTHIE

2 servings

I always loved rhubarb custard pie, and seeing fresh rhubarb at my co-op, thought "why not in a smoothie?" Although you do need to cook and cool the rhubarb first, it's not difficult and the results are wonderful—sweet and tart and bursting with flavor!

> 1¼ cups stewed rhubarb* (with its liquid)
> 4 tablespoons honey or brown rice syrup
> 1 (12.3-ounce) package soft silken tofu
> ⅔ cup dairy or dairy-free cottage or cream cheese
> 1 cup ice

Place everything in the blender container, and blend until smooth and creamy. Serve and enjoy!

Per serving: Calories 314, Protein 19 g,
Fat 6 g, Carbohydrates 6 g,
Fiber 5 g, Calcium 254 mg, Sodium 323 mg

VARIATIONS

Substitute fresh or stewed strawberries or cherries for the rhubarb, or do half rhubarb and half strawberries.

*NOTE: In order to stew the rhubarb, simply cut 2 or 3 rhubarb stems (the red part) into 1-inch pieces, and place in a pot with just enough apple juice to cover. (Discard the leaves.) Cover and bring to a low boil. Cook another 10 minutes or until the rhubarb is very tender and cooked throughout. Cool.

NewYorkCheesecake
SMOOTHIE

2 servings

Very sweet, rich, and decadent, this is great for a special occasion or romantic dinner—better, even, than the real thing.

> 1¼ cups frozen cherries
> 1¼ cups ricotta or cottage cheese, or 1 (12.3-ounce)
>   package soft silken tofu
> 2½ tablespoons dairy or dairy-free cream cheese
> 3 large graham crackers, crumbled
> 1¼ teaspoons lemon juice
> 1¼ teaspoons vanilla

Place all ingredients in the blender container, and blend until smooth and creamy. Serve, garnished perhaps with a cherry or a graham cracker. Enjoy!

Per serving: Calories 630, Protein 23 g,
Fat 28 g, Carbohydrates 76 g,
Fiber 2 g, Calcium 472 mg, Sodium 359 mg

VARIATIONS

Substitute frozen blueberries or strawberries for the cherries.

Sprinkle the top with crushed peanuts, pecans, walnuts, or hazelnuts as a garnish.

Party&Holiday
SHAKES

VeganHoliday Nog

Here's a rich eggless, dairyless variation of a holiday tradition. Keep in mind that it's still not low-fat, although there is no cholesterol and less saturated fat than regular eggnog. For a different flavor, add raspberries, strawberries, or blueberries, and omit the spices.

4 (12.3-ounce) packages soft silken tofu

4 cups soy or rice milk

½ cup honey, Sucanat, or maple syrup

½ cup safflower oil

½ teaspoon nutmeg

¼ teaspoon cinnamon

1 teaspoon vanilla

¼ teaspoon butterscotch flavoring (optional)

3 ounces rum (optional)

Blend all the ingredients together well until frothy, and chill for 15 to 30 minutes. Serve with a cinnamon stick and enjoy!

Per serving: Calories 423, Protein 15 g,
Fat 28 g, Carbohydrates 32 g,
Fiber 4 g, Calcium 74 mg, Sodium 36 mg

CherryVanillaCreme
FRAPPÉ

2 servings

For Valentine's Day or just because any day is special, share this with someone you love. Show them you care. They'll be very glad you did, and so will you.

1 cup frozen cherries
1 cup dairy or dairy-free frozen dessert or yogurt
1 can natural cherry vanilla creme soda
1 teaspoon vanilla

Place all the ingredients into the blender, and blend well. Serve in a frosted goblet or wine glass. Top with a little dairy or vegan whipped cream and a fresh cherry. Share and enjoy!

Per serving: Calories 355, Protein 4 g,
Fat 8 g, Carbohydrates 66 g,
Fiber 1 g, Calcium 116 mg, Sodium 46 mg

VARIATIONS

Try other sodas: black cherry, cherry cola, raspberry, etc.

Substitute other frozen fruit: raspberries, strawberries, etc.

HawaiianBreeze Piña-ColadaSMOOTHIE

2 servings

Sip this slowly with your eyes closed and feel the sea breezes! Wear your best Hawaiian shirt (or a grass skirt) and throw a party! Blend together well and serve in a tall, frosted glass. Aloha!

1 cup frozen pineapple juice concentrate
1 cup frozen orange juice concentrate
2 frozen bananas
1 cup coconut milk
2 ounces rum (optional)

Per serving: Calories 824, Protein 9 g,
Fat 27 g, Carbohydrates 148 g,
Fiber 7 g, Calcium 130 mg, Sodium 25 mg

CaribbeanEggNOG

2 servings

Here's an interesting twist on an old favorite—and it's vegan as well! Serve this as a refreshing change at your next winter gathering. Blend the ingredients well and garnish with a mint sprig or a cinnamon stick.

2 (12.3-ounce) packages soft silken tofu
1 (15-ounce) can coconut milk
2½ cups dairy or dairy-free milk
⅔ cup dairy or dairy-free cream cheese
1¼ teaspoons vanilla
½ teaspoon nutmeg
2 ounces rum (optional)

Per serving: Calories 522, Protein 18 g,
Fat 45 g, Carbohydrates 16 g,
Fiber 3 g, Calcium 285 mg, Sodium 213 mg

SmoothiePOWER

DancingStarSMOOTHIE

2 servings

The bubbles in this refreshing smoothie twinkle and dance like light little stars, thus the name. This is another good party beverage, sure to please, with the champagne or with sparkling juice.

> **1 cup dairy or dairy-free yogurt or buttermilk**
> **2 cups frozen raspberries or strawberries**
> **1 cup champagne or sparkling juice**
> **Pinch of nutmeg**

Blend well and serve with a sprig of mint and a lime slice. Enjoy!

Per serving: Calories 220, Protein 8 g,
Fat 3 g, Carbohydrates 24 g,
Fiber 8 g, Calcium 267 mg, Sodium 94 mg

Raspberry-PeachBlush SMOOTHIE

Flavorful and festive, serve this at your next potluck, with or without the wine! If you like, serve it in the punch bowl with frozen raspberries floating in it. Blend the ingredients well and serve. Enjoy!

> **1 cup frozen raspberries**
> **1 cup frozen peaches**
> **1 cup Zinfandel or other light white wine,**
>   **or 1 cup apple juice**

Per serving: Calories 171, Protein 2 g,
Fat 0 g, Carbohydrates 24 g,
Fiber 7 g, Calcium 29 mg, Sodium 6 mg

Pineapple-Tangerine
MARGARITA

2 servings

This makes a refreshing cooler with or without the tequila. Make lots and have a fiesta! Blend the ingredients together well, and serve immediately in a frosted margarita glass.

> **1 cup tangerine juice**
> **1 cup frozen pineapple, or ½ cup fresh pineapple chunks and ½ cup ice**
> **1 cup frozen orange juice concentrate**
> **2 teaspoons lime juice**
> **⅛ teaspoon mild chili powder**
> **2 ounces tequila (optional)**

Per serving: Calories 318, Protein 4 g,
Fat 1 g, Carbohydrates 77 g,
Fiber 2 g, Calcium 74 mg, Sodium 6 mg

HotTomato COOLER

2 servings

A cool variation on the Bloody Mary cocktail and another great party refresher! Blend everything together and serve in a chilled cocktail glass.

> **2 cups pure tomato or vegetable juice**
> **1 cup ice**
> **2 ounces vodka or gin (optional)**
> **1 teaspoon lime juice (optional)**
> **Dash of Tabasco or other hot sauce**

Per serving: Calories 41, Protein 2 g,
Fat 0 g, Carbohydrates 10 g,
Fiber 1 g, Calcium 22 mg, Sodium 876 mg

SangriaSMOOTHIE

Here's all the reason you need to throw a Southwestern fiesta. Hang a piñata, put some salsa music on the stereo and salsa dip (and tortilla chips) on the table, and, of course, pitchers of this thick, fruity sangria!

1 cup frozen raspberries
1 cup frozen pineapple
1 cup frozen mango
1 (12-ounce) package frozen orange juice concentrate
½ cup lemon or lime juice
1 bottle dry red wine (such as Burgundy or Chianti)

Blend together all the ingredients in two or three batches, and store the extra (if any) in the freezer until needed. Serve in frosted glasses and enjoy!

Per serving: Calories 139, Protein 2 g,
Fat 0 g, Carbohydrates 35 g,
Fiber 3 g, Calcium 28 mg, Sodium 3 mg

VARIATIONS

If you prefer, substitute grape juice for the wine.

Substitute juice for the frozen fruit, and add a cup or two of ice.

StrawberryKahlúa
SHAKE

2 servings

Rich and creamy, this delicious smoothie calls you to celebrate something, anything!

1 cup frozen strawberries
1 cup dairy or dairy-free frozen dessert or yogurt,
vanilla or coffee
1 cup dairy or dairy-free milk or yogurt
2 ounces Kahlua

Blend together well and serve in a tall, chilled glass with, perhaps, a dollop of dairy or vegan whipped cream. Enjoy!

Per serving: Calories 233, Protein 8 g,
Fat 11 g, Carbohydrates 26 g,
Fiber 2 g, Calcium 259 mg, Sodium 107 mg

VARIATIONS

Use frozen cherries, raspberries, or peaches instead of strawberries.

Omit the Kahlúa and add ½ cup strong regular or decaf coffee or grain beverage.

Banana-Brandy-
Amazake SMOOTHIE

2 servings

This is a nice smoothie for relaxing with friends in the evening. Put on some nice jazz or soft tunes and set out a bowl of fresh fruit.

2 cups amazake
1 cup rice milk
3 frozen bananas
2 ounces brandy
½ cup ice (optional)

Blend together well and serve in a frosted glass.
Enjoy!

Per serving: Calories 339, Protein 3 g,
Fat 2 g, Carbohydrates 65 g,
Fiber 4 g, Calcium 24 mg, Sodium 47 mg

VARIATIONS

Substitute plum wine or hard apple cider for the brandy.

Add ½ cup of your favorite frozen fruit.

Index

agave nectar 24
almond milk 23-24
 Cinnamon Roll Smoothie 36
 Sunflower Seed-Oat Bran Smoothie 88
 Triple-A Smoothie 81
almond
 -Apricot-Orange Smoothie 50
 -Ginger Smoothie 56
 Lassi 63
 Orange Joy 73
amazake 22, 24
 Banana-Brandy-Amazake Smoothie 123
 Moroccan Orange Smoothie 61
 Rice-Coconut Frappé 78
apples, buying, preparing, and storing 10
 Apple Pie Shake 96
 Cinnamon Roll Smoothie 36
 '50s Fruit Salad Smoothie 43
 Triple-A Smoothie 81
apricot(s), buying, preparing, and storing 11
 -Almond-Orange Smoothie 50
 -Banana Frappé 75
 -Ginger Smoothie 94
 -Nextarine Smoothie 49
Arctic Forest Frappé 106
Arizona Heatwave Smoothie 67
avocados, buying, preparing, and storing 11
 Avo-Banana Whip 40
 Triple-A Smoothie 81
bananas, buying, preparing, and storing 11-12
 Apricot-Banana Frappé 75
 Apricot-Ginger Smoothie 94
 Apricot-Nectarine Smoothie 49
 Arizona Heatwave Smoothie 67
 Avo-Banana Whip 40
 Banana Blizzard Shake 107
 Banana-Brandy-Amazake Smoothie 123
 Banana-Cappuccino Froth 71
 Betty Carotene Cooler 92
 Black Forest Shake 107
 Black and Blue(Berry) Smoothie 51
 Cookies & Cream Shake 97
 Figgy-Flax Frappé 87
 Funky Monkey Smoothie 99
 Mega Smoothie 89
 PB&J Smoothie 36
 Piña-Colada Smoothie 118
 Pistachio-Banana Smoothie 48
 Power Breakfast Smoothie 37
 Runner's High Protein Power Surge 86
 Sonoran Cinnamon Silence 70
 Southwest Smoothie 66
 Strawberry-Kiwi Frappé 34
 Sunflower Seed-Oat Bran Smoothie 88
 Tooty-Fruity Smoothie 41
 Tropical Strawberry Smoothie 72
 Tummy-Soothing Smoothie 91

bee pollen 26
 Power Breakfast Smoothie 37
 Strawberry-Kiwi Frappé 34
bell peppers
 High C's Smoothie 87
berries, buying, preparing, and storing 12. See also specific berries
Betty Carotene Cooler 92
bilberries 12
 Bilberry-Pear Smoothie 46
Black Cow 111
Black Forest Shake 107
blackstrap molasses 24
blenders 29-30
Bloody Mary Cooler 120
blueberries
 Arctic Forest Frappé 106
 Blueberry Bubble 98
 Black and Blue Berry Smoothie 51
blue-green algae 26
Brandy-Banana-Amazake Smoothie 123
brown rice syrup 24
buttermilk
 Arctic Forest Frappé 106
 Frappé, Peachy 79
 Mega Smoothie 89
Butterscotch Shake 102
Candy Bar Shake 112
cantaloupes, buying, preparing, and storing 12-13
 Betty Carotene Cooler 92
 Cantaloupe-Melon Cooler 76
 Tummy-Soothing Smoothie 91
carob 27
 Banana Blizzard Shake 107
 Black Forest Shake 107
 Carob Malt 110
 Carob-Mint Spirulina Smoothie 90
 Cherry Frappé 108
 Funky Monkey Smoothie 99
 Peanut Butter Twist Smoothie 100
carrots, buying, preparing, and storing 13
 Moroccan Delight Smoothie 61
carrot juice
 Betty Carotene Cooler 92
 High C's Smoothie 87
 Mega Smoothie 89
 Peppermit-Coconut-Carrot Frappé 83
 Pirate's Parrot Juice 44
cashews
 Cashew-Vanilla Smoothie 84
 Funky Monkey Smoothie 99
 Fuzzy Navel Smoothie 33
chai tea 27
 Peach Chai Smoothie 81
 Rainbow's End Smoothie 58
champagne
 Dancing Star Smoothie 119
Cheesecake Smoothie 114
cherries, buying, preparing, and storing 13
 Black Forest Shake 107

SmoothiePOWER

cherries (continued)
    Cheesecake Smoothie 114
    Cherry Frappé 108
    Cherry Vanilla Creme Frappé 117
    Ruby Tuesday Smoothie 44
chile, as a seasoning for smoothies 26
    Arizona Heatwave Smoothie 67
    Spicy Lassi 64
chocolate and cocoa 27
    Banana Blizzard Shake 107
    Black Cow 111
    Black Forest Shake 107
    Chocolate Malt 110
    Funky Monkey Smoothie 99
    Mocha Cooker 35
    Peanut Butter Twist Smoothie 100
chocolate, white
    -Hazelnut Frappé 109
Cinnamon Roll Smoothie 36
Cinnamon Silence 70
coconut milk
    Caribbean Egg Nog 118
    Orange Almond Joy 73
    Peanut Butter Twist Smoothie 100
    Peppermint-Coconut-Carrot Frappé 83
    Rice-Coconut Frappé 78
    Savory Coconut-Mint Lassi 62
    Tahitian Sunrise Breakfast Smoothie 32
    Tropical Strawberry Smoothie 72
coconuts, buying, preparing, and storing 14
    Coconut Cream Pie Shake 105
Code Red Smoothie 42
coffee 27
    Banana-Cappuccino Froth 71
    Coffee-Date Smoothie 35
    Mocha Cooler 35
    Peach Cappuccino Smoothie 38
Cookies & Cream Shake 97
Coronado's Golden Dream 68
cottage cheese
    Cheesecake Smoothie 114
    Peachy Buttermilk Frappé 79
    Rhubarb Custard Smoothie 113
cranberries, buying, preparing, and storing 14
    Cran-Raspberry Whip 74
cream cheese (dairy or dairy-free)
    Caribbean Egg Nog 118
    Cheesecake Smoothie 114
    Rhubarb Custard Smoothie 113
cucumbers
    Jade Dynasty Cucumber Whip 59
currants 15
Dancing Star Smoothie 119
dates, buying, preparing, and storing 15
    Coffee-Date Smoothie 35
    Sweet Date Shake 57
dessert shakes and smoothies 95-114
dried fruit, using 8-10
echinacea 27
    Echinacea-Lemon-Ginger Immune Builder 93

Egg Nog, Caribbean 118
Egg Nog, Vegan 116
entertaining, drinks for 115-123
equipment for making smoothies 28-30
'50s Fruit Salad Smoothie 43
figs, buying, preparing, and storing 15
    -Flax Frappé 87
    Smoothie 47
flavoring extracts 25
flaxseeds and flaxseed oil 26
    Figgy-Flax Frappé 87
    Power Breakfast Smoothie 37
    Runner's High Protein Power Surge 86
    Strawberry-Kiwi Frappé 34
    Sunflower Seed-Oat Bran Smoothie 88
food processors 29
fresh fruit, using 7-8
frozen fruit, using 7-8
fruit juice concentrate 24
fruit juices 27
fruit smoothies 39-54. See also specific fruits
Funky Monkey Smoothie 99
Fuzzy Navel Smoothie 33
ginger (root), fresh 25
    Almond Smoothie 56
    -Apricot Smoothie 94
    -Lemon-Echinacea Immune Builder 93
    Thai Pineapple Smoothie 60
gingko biloba 27
ginseng 27
    Power Breakfast Smoothie 37
goldenseal 27
Golden Sunset Smoothie 111
grain beverages 28
grape juice
    PB&J Smoothie 36
    Purple Cow (or Bean) Smoothie 102
    Tooty-Fruity Smoothie 41
grapefruit, buying, preparing, and storing 16
grapes, buying, preparing, and storing 15-16
    '50s Fruit Salad Smoothie 43
green tea 27
    Power Breakfast Smoothie 37
guavas, buying, preparing, and storing 16-17
    Guava-Passion Smoothie 52
hazelnuts
    Arctic Forest Frappé 106
    Hazelnut Torte Shake 100
    White Chocolate-Hazelnut Frappé 109
healing smoothies 85-94
herbs in smoothies 26
High C's Smoothie 87
holiday drinks 115-123
honey 25
honeydews, buying, preparing, and storing 12-13
    Betty Carotene Cooler 92
    Honeydew-Mint Cooler 52
Hot Tomato Cooler 120
Jade Dynasty Cucumber Whip 59

Jasmine Apple Smoothie 58
Kahlúa Strawberry Shake 122
kefir 23
 Avo-Banana Whip 40
 Peach Chai Smoothie 81
Key Lime Whip 72
kiwis, buying, preparing, and storing 17
 Avocado-Banana Whip 40
 Coronado's Golden Dream 68
 High C's Smoothie 87
 Kiwi-Lime Whip 101
 Strawberry-Kiwi Frappé 34
 Tropical Strawberry Smoothie 72
 Tummy-Soothing Smoothie 91
Lassi
 Almond (dairy-free) 63
 Coconut-Mint 62
 Spicy 64
Lemon-Ginger-Echinacea Immune Builder 93
Lemon-Peppermint Smoothie 53
lemons, buying, preparing, and storing 17
limes, buying, preparing, and storing 17
 -Kiwi Whip 101
 Whip 72
malt powder 25
 Chocolate (or Carob) Malt 110
 Strawberry Malt 98
mangoes, buying, preparing, and storing 18
 Arizona Heatwave Smoothie 67
 Coronado's Golden Dream 68
 Mango Lassi 65
 Mega Smoothie 89
 Rainbow's End Smoothie 58
 Raspberry-Orange Jubilation 54
 Southwest Smoothe 66
 Tahitian Sunrise Breakfast Smoothie 32
 Tucson Tonic 42
Manzanos 11
maple syrup 25
 Maple-Butter Pecan Frappé 112
 Maple-Pecan Shake 103
Mega Smoothie 89
Midnight Snack Smoothie 82
milk (dairy/nondairy) 22-24, 30
milk-based smoothies (dairy/nondairy) 69-84
Mint-Honeydew Cooler 52
Mocha Cooler 35
Moroccan Delight Smoothie 61
nectarines, buying, preparing, and storing 18
 -Apricot Smoothie 49
nondairy "milks" 22-24, 30
nonfat milk powder 23
nut butters 28
nut "milk" 22
nutritional additives 26-27
nutritional analyses of the recipes 30
nuts and seeds for smoothies 28
oat bran 26
 Sunflower Seed Smoothie 88

Oatmeal Cookie Shake 97
oat milk 23
 Cinnamon Roll Smoothie 36
 Sunflower Seed-Oat Bran Smoothie 88
omega-3 and omega-6 fatty acids 26
orange juice
 Apricot-Almond-Orange Smoothie 50
 Moroccan Orange Smoothie 61
 Orange Almond Joy 73
 Orange Juice-Wheatgrass Smoothie 92
 Orange-Tangerine Smoothie 40
 Raspberry-Orange Jubilation 54
oranges, buying, preparing, and storing 19
organic foods 9-10
 cocoa powder 27
 dairy products 22
 fruit 8-9
 juices 28
papaya(s), buying, preparing, and storing 19
 Creamsicle Smoothie 80
passionfruit 19
 Passion-Guava Smoothie 52
PB&J Smoothie 36
Peach Chai Smoothie 81
peach(es), buying, preparing, and storing 11
 Buttermilk Frappé 79
 Cappuccino Smoothie 38
 '50s Fruit Salad Smoothie 43
 Fuzzy Navel Smoothie 33
 Golden Sunset Smoothie 111
 Raspberry Blush Smoothie 119
peanut butter
 PB&J Smoothie 36
 Peanut Butter Twist Smoothie 100
pears, buying, preparing, and storing 10
 -Bilberry Smoothie 46
 Pirate's Parrot Juice 44
 Whip 71
pecans
 Cinnamon Roll Smoothie 36
 Maple-Pecan Shake 103
Peppermint-Coconut-Carrot Frappé 83
Peppermint-Lemon Smoothie 53
performance-boosting smoothies 85-94
persimmon(s), buying, preparing, and storing 19
 -Cinnamon Smoothie 45
pineapples, buying, preparing, and storing 20
 Arizona Heatwave Smoothie 67
 Banana Blizzard Shake 107
 Piña-Colada Smoothie 118
 Sangria Smoothie 121
 -Tangerine Margarita 120
 Thai Ginger Smoothie 60
Pirate's Parrot Juice 44
Pistachio-Banana Smoothie 48
plums, buying, preparing, and storing 20
Power Breakfast Smoothie 37
preservatives in fruit 9
prickly pear syrup
 Southwest Smoothie 66

protein powders 26
    Blueberry Bubble 98
    Oatmeal Cookie Shake 97
    Runner's High Protein Power Surge 86
    Sunflower Seed-Oat Bran Smoothie 88
prunes, buying, preparing, and storing 20
    Oatmeal Cookie Shake 97
psyllium seed husks 26
    Figgy-Flax Frappé 87
pumpkin, buying, preparing, and storing 21
    Pie Shake 104
Purple Cow (or Bean) Smoothie 102
raisins, buying, preparing, and storing 15-16
    Cinnamon Roll Smoothie 36
raspberries
    Code Red Smoothie 42
    Cran Whip 74
    Dancing Star Smoothie 119
    -Orange Jubilation 54
    -Peach Blush Smoothie 119
    Ruby Tuesday Smoothie 44
rhubarb, buying, preparing, and storing 21
    Custard Smoothie 113
Rice-Coconut Frappé 78
rice milk 23-24. See also amazake
    Banana-Brandy-Amazake Smoothie 123
rose water 28
    Mango Lassi 65
Ruby Tuesday Smoothie 44
St. John's wort 27
Sangria Smoothie 121
smoothies, tips for making 30
sodas, natural 28
Sonoran Cinnamon Silence 70
sorbets 25
Southwest Smoothie 66
soymilk 23-24
soy yogurt 22
spices for smoothies 25-26
Spicy Lassi 64
spirulina 26
    Carob-Mint Smoothie 90
    Power Breakfast Smoothie 37
stewed fruit, using 8-10
strawberries, buying, preparing, and storing 21
    Avo-Banana Whip 40
    Code Red Smoothie 42
    Dancing Star Smoothie 119
    Kahlúa Shake 122
    -Kiwi Frappé 34
    Malt 98
    Mega Smoothie 89
    Power Breakfast Smoothie 37
    Ruby Tuesday Smoothie 44
    Tooty-Fruity Smoothie 41
    Tropical Smoothie 72
sugar cane juice or crystals 25
sulfur dioxide in fruits 9
Sunflower Seed-Oat Bran Smoothie 88

sweet potatoes, buying, preparing, and storing 22
sweeteners 24-25
tahini
    Moroccan Orange Smoothie 61
Tahitian Sunrise Tropical Breakfast Smoothie 32
Tamarind Smoothie 41
tangerines, buying, preparing, and storing 18-19
    -Orange Smoothie 40
    -Pineapple Margarita 120
tofu 22, 24
    Caribbean Egg Nog 118
    Cheesecake Smoothie 114
    Coconut Cream Pie Shake 105
    Cran-Raspberry Whip 74
    Key Lime Whip 72
    Kiwi-Lime Whip 101
    Midnight Snack Smoothie 82
    Rhubarb Custard Smoothie 113
    Vegan Holiday Nog 116
tomato juice
    Hot Tomato Cooler 120
Tooty-Fruity Smoothie 41
Triple-A Smoothie 81
Tropical Strawberry Smoothie 72
Tucson Tonic 42
Tummy-Soothing Smoothie 91
unsulfured dried fruit 9
vanilla 26
    -Cashew Smoothie 84
    Creme Frappé, Cherry 117
Vegan Holiday Nog 116
Vita-Mix 29
watermelon, buying, preparing, and storing 22
    Cantaloupe-Melon Cooler 76
    Watermelon Smoothie 46
wheat bran and germ 27
    Apricot-Banana Frappé 75
    Black and Blue(Berry) Smoothie 51
    Figgy Figgy Smoothie 47
    Mega Smoothie 89
    Midnight Snack Smoothie 82
    PB&J Smoothie 36
    Pistachio-Banana Smoothie 48
    Runner's High Protein Power Surge 86
    Strawberry-Kiwi Frappé 34
    Sunflower Seed-Oat Bran Smoothie 88
Wheatgrass-Orange Juice Smoothie 92
white chocolate 28
    -Hazelnut Frappé 109
wine
    Dancing Star Smoothie 119
    Golden Sunset Smoothie 111
    Raspberry-Peach Blush Smoothie 119
    Sangria Smoothie 121
yam(s), buying, preparing, and storing 22
    -Orange Smoothie 77
young coconut 14
    Orange Almond Joy 73
    Raspberry-Orange Jubilation 54

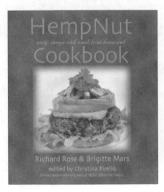